The Meaning
of David Cameron

The Meaning
of David Cameron

Richard Seymour

BOOKS

Winchester, UK
Washington, USA

The Meaning of David Cameron

First published by O-Books, 2010
O Books is an imprint of John Hunt Publishing Ltd., The Bothy, Deershot Lodge, Park Lane, Ropley,
Hants, SO24 0BE, UK
office1@o-books.net
www.o-books.com

Distribution in:	South Africa
	Stephan Phillips (pty) Ltd
UK and Europe	Email: orders@stephanphillips.com
Orca Book Services Ltd	Tel: 27 21 4489839 Telefax: 27 21 4479879
Home trade orders	Text copyright Richard Seymour 2010
tradeorders@orcabookservices.co.uk	
Tel: 01235 465521 Fax: 01235 465555	ISBN: 978 1 84694 456 7
Export orders	Design: Stuart Davies
exportorders@orcabookservices.co.uk	
Tel: 01235 465516 or 01235 465517	All rights reserved. Except for brief quotations
Fax: 01235 465555	in critical articles or reviews, no part of this
	book may be reproduced in any manner
USA and Canada	without prior written permission from the
NBN	publishers.
custserv@nbnbooks.com	
Tel: 1 800 462 6420 Fax: 1 800 338 4550	The rights of Richard Seymour as author have
	been asserted in accordance with the
Australia and New Zealand	Copyright, Designs and Patents Act 1988.
Brumby Books	
sales@brumbybooks.com.au	A CIP catalogue record for this book is
Tel: 61 3 9761 5535 Fax: 61 3 9761 7095	available from the British Library.
Far East (offices in Singapore, Thailand,	
Hong Kong, Taiwan)	
Pansing Distribution Pte Ltd	Printed in the UK by CPI Antony Rowe
kemal@pansing.com	Printed in the USA by Offset Paperback Mfrs,
Tel: 65 6319 9939 Fax: 65 6462 5761	Inc

We operate a distinctive and ethical publishing philosophy in all
areas of its business, from its global network of authors to
production and worldwide distribution.

CONTENTS

Acknowledgments

This book had of necessity to be written quickly, and I am indebted to a number of people who helped me through the process. Corey Robin generously discussed his ideas on conservatism at length with me, and provided numerous references and articles. His forthcoming book on conservatism and counterrevolution is likely to be essential reading. Jeremy Gilbert was very helpful in providing clarification on issues related to social democracy and the transition to neoliberalism, and went out of his way to provide numerous references and detailed explanations. Many, many thanks to both. Thanks also to Alex Andrews, who provided some very useful resources on the strange thought-world of the 'Red Tories'. I am also grateful to Tariq Godard for giving me the idea of this book and encouraging me to write it, and to Mark Fisher for helping edit the final manuscript. Lastly, perhaps most importantly, my thanks and love must go to Marie, whose ideas I stole.

Prologue

David Cameron is not so much the subject of this book as the occasion for it. Cameron is of little interest, except as a cipher, a sort of nonentity who channels the prevailing *geist*. The real subjects of this book are the historical forces galvanising the Tory leadership – not only the immediate crises of war and recession, but the deep structural transformations that have taken place in the UK in the generation since the zenith of Thatcherism. These changes, in class and gender relations, in the underlying economic structure, and in the norms of respectable political discourse, have given us the chimera of Cameronism. But the same processes that have offered the Tories the chance of office could also sideline them for a generation. For, as resourcefully and ruthlessly as they exploit the opportunities they are presented with, the alliance of shifty neocons, Tory 'wets' and upper class Thatcherites-in-drag that currently hold precarious tenure over their party are as apt to be ground under the wheel of history as they are to be elevated by it.

How the Tories became 'progressive'
The Conservative Party under David Cameron represents itself as a 'progressive' force in British politics, concerned with gender equality, civil liberties and the rising inequality of wealth. [1] To this end, in addition to the usual run of Tory think-tanks such as Policy Exchange and the Centre for Policy Studies which helped popularise Thatcherite ideas in the run-up to 1979, the Centre for Social Justice has been launched by Ian Duncan Smith to address the problems of poverty, discrimination and inequality from a conservative perspective.

The centrepiece of the Tory campaign is a 'revolt' against 'Big Government' in favour of 'Big Society', which the party claims can more effectively deliver public services and welfare systems than the state. In this vein, Cameron has also adopted the theme of 'compassionate conservatism' first vaunted by George W Bush's election campaign in 2000, taking advice from Bush's mentor Marvin Olasky. The logic of 'compassionate conservatism' is that private charity is superior to state welfare systems because the former provides the possibility of a transformative personal interaction that state bureaucracies don't offer. The soft sell to one side, the net effect of putting this philosophy into practise can already be seen in America. Food lines and soup kitchens provide inadequate sustenance for the 'working poor' and unemployed, while corporations and the wealthy pay lower taxes than they have for generations.

In its first appearance, the new Tory doctrine focused on the gulf between the apparent material prosperity of society and the examples of supposed social breakdown foregrounded by the media – binge drinking, violent crime, anti-social behaviour and broken families. Money, the Tories maintained, had not made for spiritual well-being. The recession that was heralded by the financial collapse beginning in late 2007, and the debt incurred by the government as a result of bank bailouts and falling tax receipts, gave the Conservatives the opportunity to demand public spending cuts. But even as they pledged to cut public sector pay, slash spending and cap pensions, they assured public sector workers that it didn't matter because years of pay increases and higher spending had failed to make them happier. Only liberation from the encroachments of bureaucracy, the freedom to pursue targets by whatever means they deem fit, could restore their creative capacity and their lost sense of self-esteem. Targets, backed up by performance-related pay, would free the public sector workers.[2]

This curious conception of freedom was explored in Adam Curtis' documentary *The Trap*. It is based on a deeply misanthropic view of humanity elaborated during the Cold War and subsequently championed by the New Right, in which human beings are held to be inherently uncooperative, back-stabbing, and self-aggrandising. The public service ethic, in this view, is organised hypocrisy, a cognitive script that masks self-interest and generates inefficiency. Only by allowing people to be selfish, and using their self-interest to incentivise the required outcomes, could efficiency and morale be restored. As I will argue later, this strange conceit has far deeper roots in conservative thought than Curtis suggests.

New Labour's supporters are quick to point out how incongruous the Tories' 'progressive' branding is, sometimes in exhausting detail. The Tories, they note, remain traditionalist on marriage, are opposed to multiculturalism, propose tax breaks for corporations and the rich, oppose the EU from the right and find their natural allies in Europe among anti-Semites and homophobes, and propose rapid, deep public spending cuts to pay for the bankers' bail-out. David Cameron, trading heavily on ignorance about his recent past, depicts himself as the man who transformed the Conservative Party into a 'radical' force. This from a professed Thatcherite, an opponent of multiculturalism and immigration, a supporter of the 'war on terror' who has promoted a coterie of neoconservatives to his shadow cabinet, an oblocutor of trade union 'militants' who advocates low taxes for businesses and the wealthy, a staunch royalist, and a supporter of 'family values' who wants to curtail abortion rights and voted in favour of legislation preserving Section 28. Progress indeed, if the benchmark is 1834.[3]

Yet this is one point on which New Labour apologists have no right to crow, as their party bears substantial responsibility for this state of affairs. No party did more to capture such terms as 'progressive' and 'radical' for a right-wing agenda than the Labour Party under Tony Blair. This is a government that has presided over the aggressive privatisation of public services, whether directly or through treasury-draining Private Finance Initiatives; tax cuts for corporations; reduced inheritance tax and capital gains tax; and tax reforms benefiting shareholders. The Tories have been able to capitalise on the fact that income inequality after more than a decade of Labour government was higher than at any point since records began in 1961, beating the record set by the Conservatives under Thatcher.[4]

At the same time, New Labour's refusal to endorse redistribution and the focus on 'social exclusion' – by no means incompatible with the Tories' agenda – has led to a decline in support for egalitarian politics.[5] And, though the recession has made the financiers empowered by Thatcher extremely unpopular, the Tories are less vulnerable to criticism of their City ties because Labour itself relaxed City regulations to such an extent that the square mile became known as "Wall Street's Guantanamo", because US investors could get away with practises in London that were forbidden in New York. Brown later admitted that he had been lobbied by the bankers to reduce regulations.[6]

Internationally, New Labour was far more vigorous in pursuing the Atlantic alliance, and joining in American wars, than its predecessors ever were. It was Blair who promulgated the doctrine of the 'international community' that rationalised the wars pursued first by Clinton and then by Bush, and who played the greatest part in reviving the tradition of 19th Century liberal imperialism. Similarly, in Europe, it was under Blair's watch that Britain allied with figures from the hard right such as Berlusconi and Sarkozy, precisely because of their support for Washington and unpopular measures such as the Giscard d'Estaing drafted EU Treaty.

The moral alarmism of the Conservative Party also has an alibi in New Labour policy. New Labour with its mean, vindictive streak, increased the prison population to crisis levels, and dreamed up ever more inventive ways of punishing people, even where they had committed no crime – ASBOs being an outrageous case in point. It was New Labour, with its incessant moralising, that pioneered the idea of pre-emptively intervening

4

in families deemed likely to fail and produce socially dysfunctional offspring, thus providing many of the materials from which the moral panic about 'broken Britain' was constructed. The Tories can only outflank Labour to the left on the issue of civil liberties, for example on ID cards, because New Labour's fanatical authoritarianism has outraged even traditionalist conservatives.

The consensus on multiculturalism and anti-racism which had constrained Tory administrations was attacked by New Labour from its first term. It was Jack Straw, as Home Secretary, who vilified gypsies and set up a network of detention centres for asylum seekers that went further than even the obdurate Michael Howard had dared. It was David Blunkett who demanded that British Asians should speak English in their own homes, proposed a 'Britishness test' for immigrants, and signalled the end of 'multiculturalism'. It was New Labour-friendly intellectuals, such as David Goodhart and Trevor Phillips, who provided a neo-Powellite rationale for this shift. And it was Tony Blair who, in his last days as Prime Minister, blamed a spate of gun and knife crime in the capital on 'black culture', drawing from the culturalist racism of the New Right. Blair, of whom Cameron is so emulous, was an instinctive Tory who drove the country harder and farther to the right than the administration he defeated in 1997 – all under the inscription of 'progress'. Sycophantic toward the wealthy, ingratiating toward Her Majesty, fawning over Bush – the only people who really inspired Blair's disgust were the poor and weak, and those residual "forces of conservatism" in his own party who challenged him, meekly, from the Left.

The grammar of 'progressive' Toryism would not even be intelligible were it not for New Labour. However, New Labour itself is a project that was only possible because of fundamental changes to Britain's socio-political landscape, and because of global metamorphoses that altered the terms of political discourse. The Thatcherite attack on organised labour in the 1980s, involving the provocation and defeat of major national strikes, and the sacrifice of manufacturing jobs to the gods of NAIRU, recomposed society in a dramatic way. Atrophying militant working class strongholds depleted the Left's social base, empowered the right-wing in the Labour Party and trade union bureaucracy, and ultimately squeezed even those on Labour's soft-left who had cheered on the homophobic attacks on Peter Tatchell, the witch-hunts against Militant, and the embrace of 'free market' economics.

The Thatcher government's creation of a debt/speculation economy provided an illusion of economic well-being, even as the permanent army of unemployed labour remained well above, and growth well below, that of previous generations. By rationing housing and privatising council stock, the Tories ensured that homeowners would see the value of their properties soar. As wages were no longer to rise in proportion with productivity, the fact that people could borrow against their property would ensure that consumption remained robust. This made enough people feel wealthy enough, despite the insecurity of their new assets, to maintain a Tory plurality throughout the 1980s and force Labour to adapt.

Coterminous with the grave defeats inflicted on organised labour in the 1980s, the fall of the USSR – though hardly a regrettable fact in itself – contributed to a collapse in faith in the idea of historical progress. The belief that history had any discernable direction toward the greater liberty and equality of humankind had been under attack as part of an intellectual reaction, sometimes misleadingly labelled 'postmodernism', since the late 1970s. The incredulity toward those 'grand narratives' that could possibly underpin the idea of progress was apparently vindicated by the sudden absence of the 'Second World', an historical de-materialism that was more farcical than tragic. 'Progress', in a vista lacking an alternative to capitalism, could come to mean

6

simply adapting oneself to changes wrought by market competition, however baleful they were. The embrace of 'progress' by the Conservative Party is merely a logical, if perverse, corollary of this development. In order to pick apart the mesh of mystifications made possible by such inversions, therefore, it is necessary to examine Cameronism in an historical light, and particularly in light of a lost referent of political discourse: class.

The case for 'class war'

The Conservative Party has always had to reach out beyond its class base to win elections. In its first incarnation as the party of agrarian capital and the landed gentry, before the working class had obtained the franchise, it had find a way to appeal to industrial capital or risk being consigned to oblivion. This was Robert Peel's task when the Tories first governed as Conservatives, a name derived from the French term 'conservateur'. The Great Reform Act of 1832 had removed votes from many of the 'rotten boroughs' that had guaranteed artificially large majorities for the Tories' rural base, while awarding votes to new industrial cities that had emerged as British industrial capitalism took off after rebuffing the Napoleonic threat. It was Peel, himself a venture capitalist who had funded the development of the 'Spinning Jenny', who worked hardest to reconcile the Tories to the changed law and prove to emerging urban capitalists that the party could be a natural home for them. By the latter half of the 19th Century, they were enjoying some success in this.

Similarly, when the Second Reform Act of 1867 enfranchised the majority of adult working class males (in a manner quite unintended by Disraeli, who had drafted the Act to counter Liberal and radical pressure for more democratising changes), the Tories adapted by developing constituency associations to recruit members and mobilise middle class voters, though members in fact had little say in the party's governance. Throughout the 20th Century, the Tories became the party of industrial capital as the Liberals were eclipsed by the ascent of mass social democracy and agrarian capital entered into precipitous decline. However, in addition to capitalists and the middle classes, for electoral purposes they have usually been able to win over approximately one third of the working class.[7] The class basis of the Conservative Party, together with its assiduous electoral coalition-building, is essential to explaining the party's present comportment, known as 'Cameronism'.

This is unlikely to be a welcome observation among those for whom the very mention of class is at best a *faux pas*. Recall that Cameron, an offspring of the financial bourgeoisie with some royalty in his distant ancestry, is the first truly establishment Tory leader for decades. The Conservative Party has been electing leaders of comparatively plebeian origins for some four decades since the dissolution of the 'Magic Circle'.[8] That the Tories have finally overcome the taboo on ostentatious elitism is likely to result from a greater taboo on the very idea of class politics. Cameron is thus at pains to dismiss the class resentment that he and his party provoke, and which Gordon Brown clumsily tried to capitalise on by satirising Cameron's Eton pedigree, as "petty" and "spiteful". It is only fair to add that some New Labour ministers are also palpably embarrassed by the idea of such "class war".[9]

The taboo over the issue of class has generated a censorious political language: the slightest intimation that class is an issue is self-righteously denounced as 'the politics of envy'. This reached an absurd apotheosis when, during the 'expenses scandal' that inconvenienced parliamentarians in 2009, Tory MP Anthony Steen responded to criticism of his lavish expenses claims by saying that the public were simply "jealous" of his "very, very large house".[10] And in general, the Tories are very reluctant to concede that there is anything wrong with class privilege, even where it hurts them electorally. At one point, it was reported that nineteen of twenty-nine members of the shadow cabinet were millionaires. It was a year before Cameron let it be known that he was ordering them to give up the lucrative jobs that had made them millionaires.[11]

But perhaps we will be spared the gasps of affronted respectability and how-dare-yous on their part if I explain that by class I do not mean an incidental biographical factoid. All too often, class is confused with a lifestyle, or with status, or with some nebulously 'ethnic' trait that one associates with top hats or, conversely, cloth caps and sentimental reminiscences about the East End. Class is not a status, a lifestyle, a culture or an ethnicity. And it does not, contra the poetasters of 'the white working class', have a colour. By class, I simply mean the relationship between the minority who own the lion's share of wealth and capital, and the majority who sell their labour to get by.

By way of clarification, allow me to cite the occasion for (not subject of) this book on the defining class dispute of the Thatcher era: "The miners' strike was tragic, but ... in the end the right of management to manage and business to invest and people to go about their lives just has to win through".[12] Cameron's sentiment, whether intentionally or not, grasps the class relationship in a very concise way. The 'right' of business to invest and management to manage is, of course, no more than the privilege of a class endowed with the means to do so. The duty of workers to submit to managerial discipline and refrain from interference in investment, which is the exclusive domain of the owners of capital, is one they incur because their sole economic asset is their ability to work. In this sense, the basic class antagonism in society is defined by ownership (and lack thereof) of the means of production.[13]

Cameron uses the appropriate euphemisms – for example, one doesn't ordinarily refer to 'capitalists' or 'the ruling class' in mixed company on pain of provoking a shop-soiled 'Life of Brian' reference. The appropriate term is 'business'. Even so, the man who would rule Britannia shows that he understands the class system and his sympathies within it, as all Tory leaders must.[14] In light of this, an intelligent disrespect of the taboo on class, and the evasions of the major parties on the issue, is surely called for. In this spirit, I will cheerfully grate sensibilities by referring throughout this book to such apparently dated notions as workers, capitalists and class struggle. If it is any consolation, I note that such concepts are at least as modern as the Mandevillian tenets upon which defenders of the 'free market' stake their case.

Meritocracy: a hegemonic language for the ruling class

One reason it is important to take class seriously is that there is a cross-party consensus in favour of 'meritocracy'. This is an under-defined idea, for there is no shared conception of what 'merit' is. If people or their actions are meritorious, deserving reward, they are so because of a broader conception of what constitutes a good society – a moral philosophy, or a theory of justice. And as Alasdair Macintyre points out, "every moral philosophy presupposes a sociology". In order to understand the politics of meritocracy, it is therefore necessary to unpack the idea a little, examine its constituents, and see how they relate to the sociology of late capitalism. This, we will do in more detail in Chapter Two, but for now it will suffice to say that it is most cognate with a conservative moral philosophy valuing hierarchy and inequality. And in practise it serves as a language of class domination, insofar as merit is implicitly judged by outcomes (of wealth and status) rather than the processes that led to them.

For all this, meritocracy is an idea that, having initially been a dystopian horror in the hands of its author, Michael Young, has become hegemonic. It was floated as mood music for the 1979 electoral campaign by the Thatcherite wing of the Conservative Party who summarised the doctrine as 'equal rights to become unequal'. It went on to become the signature tune of the

Thatcher era. But it became hegemonic when the idea was embraced by New Labour – originally in its 'Commission for Social Justice', which dropped egalitarian politics for meritocracy. Rather than explicitly seeking to redistribute wealth, it would seek to tackle those forms of "social exclusion" which prevented people from having access to the meritocratic order. Rather than attacking the privilege of the rich, it would value them as "wealth creators" and seek to include them in policymaking, including in the formulation of policies designed to assist the poor.

David Cameron, despite having benefited from the affir-mative-action-for-rich-white-males known as class privilege, is an avowed 'meritocrat'. The conviction with which he upbraids the "state knows best, know your place, rigid, class system" (fluent Blairese) confirms it.[15] The class system, in this view, is the antithesis of a meritocracy wherein a person is empowered to fully exercise her own talents and reap the full rewards of doing so, free from the constraints imposed by the state, trade unions and the old school tie. Policies are built on such premises, and the rhetoric is crafted to appeal to 'aspiring' voters – the implication of this terminology being that those who do not respond to such vulgar serenading of petit-bourgeois resentment lack aspiration.

The meritocratic credo has also generated a vocabulary which has the effect of naturalising and justifying the class system. Taxing profits, wealth and higher incomes is, for example, construed as 'punishing success'. We are told that those who have achieved through their own graft should be incentivised, not penalised, by the tax system. We can see how this argument works in practise. In 2005, the shadow chancellor George Osborne proposed investigating the benefits of a 'flat tax' system. This policy is championed by the Taxpayers' Alliance – a lobby funded by pro-Conservative businessmen, and a source of many of Osborne's policy ideas – on the grounds that it is both more efficient, and fairer in that it incentivises success rather than punishing it.[16] The proposal for a flat income tax, to be set at approximately 22% of personal income for everyone earning more than £15,000, was rejected by the Tory pioneer of 'flatter' taxes, Brian Reading, on the grounds that it would benefit only the top 10% of income earners and create 27 million losers, and would be "political suicide".[17] Osborne therefore declined to pursue that option, but instead set up a Tax Reform Commission to consider the effects of some proposed Tory policies designed to create a "flatter" tax system.[18]

The first policy, the abolition of inheritance tax, was shown by the commission to benefit only the wealthiest 6% of estates. Nevertheless, the Tories proposed to raise the inheritance tax threshold so that only those with assets over £1m would pay it. New Labour responded by raising the tax-free threshold for married couples to £650,000. By 2009, it was reported that the number of households paying inheritance tax was down to 12,000, a record low. Another policy, the abolition of capital gains tax, was again found to be most likely to benefit the wealthy, as the main asset possessed by the majority of people is their home which is already exempt from capital gains tax. The Tories nonetheless pushed for a reduction in capital gains tax. And again, New Labour sought to seize Conservative territory by introducing reductions on the tax paid by 'entrepreneurs' and speculators.[19]

These policies, as their framers surely understood, benefit only the capitalist class. They may inspire some people to wish that they themselves were wealthy, but they are not part of a programme that would enable the required social mobility. As policymakers must also know, few of those who succeed do so without the resources that class privilege endow, and none do so without enabling structures and happy accidents propelling their ascent. The 'self-made man' is roughly on a par with Sasquatch – many claim to have seen him, and some credulous media outlets purport to have proof of his existence, but this *meritofaunæ cryptid* is assuredly folklore. Social immobility remains as entrenched as it was more than a generation ago, as the resources required to succeed in a capitalist society continue to be largely transmitted through inheritance. [20] What is more, the language of meritocracy seems designed to ensure that this remains the case.

The case for 'apathy': technocracy and the erosion of democracy

Of course, the value of 'meritocracy' is not the only area in which there is a cross-party consensus. All three major parties, for example, agree on the need to privatise state assets, maintain a free market, reduce the size of the welfare state, and raise the state pension age. This consensus is all the more striking because of the unpopularity of these policies. Of note in the 2010 election, having unanimously approved a bailout for the banks, not one of the parties opposes record public spending cuts to pay for the deficit partially created by it. In global terms, they are all committed to Atlanticism, notwithstanding the Liberals' short-lived and unprincipled objection to the invasion of Iraq. They each favour the continuation of NATO, and its continued involvement in Afghanistan. As regards the EU, Cameron's acquiescence to the EU Treaty confirms that his party will pursue broadly the same approach as their opponents, pragmatically negotiating the most advantageous conditions for UK capital within a neoliberal settlement.

No wonder, then, that 'Cameronism' is so often misinterpreted as 'centrist' and 'moderate'. If all parties agree on the fundamentals of the Thatcherite agenda that David Cameron proposes, then Thatcherism is just centrist common sense as far as the political class is concerned. Politicians and pundits complain about the apparent lack of civic energy among the public. Election turnouts are demonstrating a consistent decline, and parties no longer seem able to recruit members in the numbers they once did. The 2001 election turnout was the lowest on record for a general election in the UK, and resulted in a tremendous amount of sermonising from media pulpits. 'Apathy' was the *cri de coeur*. The punters were, if I may caricature the argument a little, charged with being too absorbed in the business of acquisition and consumption to take note of the serious issues governing their life chances. Perhaps they were even too content with their lot to worry about politics – a self-aggrandising assessment for the political class. Yet, those complaining are also those who by their actions marginalise the public. The majority who oppose privatisation, or who opposed the invasion of Iraq and the on-going occupation of Afghanistan, are largely unrepresented in public debates and in parliament.

Again, the Tories have much to thank their opponents for. One of New Labour's hallmarks has been its tendency to depoliticise highly controversial matters by rendering them as technocratic problems. Thus, for example, its decision to embrace the highly expensive Private Finance Initiatives (PFIs) which they had derided in opposition, giving companies the opportunity to profit from the delivery of public services, was justified on the grounds of a fiscal imperative. The alternative to seeking investment from private capital was to borrow (since taxing the wealthy was ruled out from the beginning), and this was against economic orthodoxy. That justification was never sound – projects funded by PFI have consistently cost far more than their publicly funded equivalents. And it experienced a severe knock when the costs of PFI projects contributed partially to a fiscal crisis for the NHS in 2006.[21]

New Labour's reign has seen the proliferation of technocratic jargon, among which is the phrase "evidence based policy-making". As Tony Blair put it in the party's 1997 manifesto, "what counts is what works." As the case of Iraq demonstrates, this usually translates into policy based evidence-making. This isn't merely flippant: evidence has to be selected, weighted, and filtered for a policy to be decided on, and the criteria for the selection, weighting and filtering of evidence are likely to be determined by the policies that ministers and senior civil servants already prefer. Even so, what is important is the signal sent by such phrases. Like 'blue skies thinking' and other New Labour cynosures, the term has distinctly managerial cadences, suggesting efficient, non-ideological administration. The very idea of 'non-ideological' administration is, of course, a deeply ideological conception, akin to 'ideological baggage'. Its appearance is a sign of stultifying orthodoxy, not of intellectual suppleness.

The Tories are anxious to give the impression of breaking from the technocratic language of their opponents. This is evident in their attack on New Labour's bureaucratic centralism and demand that professionals be permitted to deliver public services as their judgment guides them. This is transparently tied to an agenda of privatisation and breaking up collective bargaining with performance related pay schemes. And the seeming deference to 'professionals' and 'experts' just is the *sine qua non* of technocracy. However, the campaign spiel recognises and responds to the growing sense that the state, far from being a forum for democratic contention, is impervious to the popular will.

It is in this light that David Cameron proposes to pass a law allowing any petition with 100,000 signatures to be formally debated in the House of Commons, whereas any petition with over 1m signatures will force a vote on legislation. [22] This is supposed to offer the electorate a way of forcing politicians to listen to them, though it is hard to see why – even if a petition did force a vote on a popular piece of legislation – MPs would not simply vote it down, ignoring public opinion in exactly the way that they ignored public opinion over Iraq. At any rate, such avenues are no match for the resourcefulness with which capital can regularly meet, lobby, subsidise and fraternise elected politicians. But, given the Cameronite emphasis on 'modern presentation', it was always predictable that the Tories would respond to the crisis of democracy by offering a simulacrum of democratisation just as they spent much of their time out of office offering a simulacrum of opposition while backing New Labour on almost every significant policy. Cameronism is just another symptom of our democratic malaise rather than a cure.

Given the way that politicians treat us, I'm not sure that a certain kind of 'apathy' isn't warranted. The stereotype of voters who were apathetic about the issues was never accurate, but there is a justifiable indifference toward the P T Barnum-esque gee-whizzery of our political class when it is soliciting our votes. In saying this, I don't mean to spread the pernicious fiction that 'all politicians are the same'. They are not, and the fascist mobil-isation in Barking and Dagenham reminds us that there are even worse things than Thatcherites with a blue or red rosette. But when the Browns, Camerons and Cleggs of this world wax wistful on the topic of voter apathy, we are surely entitled to shrug, sigh, and mutter "well, they would say that wouldn't they?" If we can be bothered, that is.

Conclusion

In the ensuing chapters, I will flesh out some of these (hopefully provocative) arguments, anatomising what I take to be the components of Cameronism, more broadly of modern conser-vatism, and also of the parlous state of democracy. I will argue that Cameron, whether he wins or loses the election (and as I write, an unexpected Liberal Democrat surge may yet deprive him of victory), is both a successful mimic of and legitimate successor to Blair. The logic of Cameronism, as with Blairism, is to consolidate the hegemony of what was in its inception a *restorationist* project, an attempt to restore the social power and profitability of capital after the turbulent Seventies by breaking the power of organised labour. This was always going to involve pacifying a restive population, narrowing the political field and marginalising the working class majority. Despite periodic bouts of popular rebellion, this project was overwhelmingly successful in its own terms, and it is ultimately responsible for today's drab, vitiated social landscape and the increasingly rarefied election spectacles in which the most important questions have already been decided.

Chapter One

'Apathy'

The revival of the Conservative Party post-2005 has typically been attributed to David Cameron's leadership, particularly his Blair-like qualities. The resemblances are superficially striking. Cameron certainly emulates Blair in his lachrymose pseudo-sincerity, his thespian attributes, his emphasis on 'modern presentation', and his eagerness to distance himself from his party base. Like Blair, he cultivates an appeal to 'aspirational' voters – he is posh, educated, ambitious, a high-flyer. No broad Yorkshire vowels or music hall paternity mar his potential appeal to professionals in key marginals. Similarly, he eschews the crass populism of his predecessors, which dismayed bourgeois liberals. And he has excelled in the art of delegating nastiness. Blair, like the Queen, always liked to give the impression of being above the squalid factional manoeuvring and media intrigues that dogged his colleagues. So it is with Cameron, who is not short of fall guys when a Tory attack goes awry.

Far deeper, though, are the political affinities which bind the major parties in a three-way consensus over the broad directions of policy. It is because of this consensus that trivial personality and presentational quirks acquire an exaggerated import. Noam Chomsky has offered the comparison with the way that brand advertising exaggerates the petty differences between one kind of toothpaste and another. They have distinctive appearances and packaging, but they each do much the same thing, and each leave you with an urge to rinse the taste out of your mouth. It is in this light that I would like to pose the question of political apathy.

The growing tendency to boycott elections has been interpreted as political indifference. Even where people seek to express political demands outside the electoral arena, as with anticapitalist and antiwar protesters, the media have often preferred to write their protests off as apolitical trouble-making.[23] Alternatively, it is asserted that the rejection of voting reflects an anti-political sentiment on the part of people who would prefer it if politicians got off their backs. Such is the sentiment that the Conservative Party has tried to convert into electoral capital in the 2010 general election. This misses the point that disengagement from electoral politics, whatever its merits as a strategy, often has clearly articulated political motives. And it is a response to the declining ability of the parliamentary system, always mandarin and aloof even in its representative capacity, to respond to popular will.

Non-voting ≠ apathy

The 2010 UK general election should see a higher turnout than previous general elections in 2001 and 2005, due to it being one of the closest for years, and particularly due to the unexpected 'surge' for the Liberal Democrats. If so, however, it will interrupt a long term trend toward disengagement from electoral politics. Until recently, non-voting in the UK was not seen as a protest. A substantial amount of non-voting was accounted for by involuntary factors, or by simple apathy. For the first time in 2001, deliberate abstention accounted for 62% of non-voting, and perhaps all of non-voting in 2005.[24]

This could perhaps be compared with the situation in the United States, where voting turnout has historically been far lower than in the UK – a 63% turnout in the 2008 presidential elections was the record high for some forty years, though it was not much greater than the record low in the UK general election in 2001, when turnout was 59%. Moreover, there is an obvious class basis for US non-voting. A comparison of voting patterns in the Sixties and early Seventies in the two countries studied the correlation between class self-identification and voting. The study found that those most likely to self-identify as working class voted Labour in the UK, but did not vote in the United States. Of those who did vote for either party in the US, barring the exception of Governor Wallace's segregationist campaign in 1968 which galvanised many poor whites, overwhelming majorities self-identified as middle class. More than two-thirds of supporters of the Democratic Party, which claims a near monopoly on all social forces left-of-centre in national elections, self-identified as middle class. Tens of millions of working class voters simply boycotted these elections.[25]

But if working class voters have historically turned out at elections to support the Labour Party, this is a trend that is beginning to erode. Labour still gains a greater proportion of support from self-identifying working class voters than any other party does, but it has suffered declining majorities in heartlands seats for more than a decade, as core Labour voters have abstained from voting. The 1997 elections which New Labour won with a 'landslide' saw what was then a record low turnout of 71%. This was particularly pronounced among working class voters. New Labour, though it had increased its support among middle class voters, had actually lost 5% of its support among working class voters. In 2001, when turnout fell to 59%, a further 2.8 million Labour voters refused to cast a vote. Once again, Labour had increased its support among middle class (professional and managerial) voters, but lost support among core working class voters, especially manual workers and 'unskilled' labourers.[26]

In 2005, Labour lost another million voters. Using the 'social class' classifications beloved of pollsters and market researchers, research determined that Labour had increased its support among AB voters (professionals, managers and supervisors) by 2% since 1997. However, it had lost its support among every other group, particularly among voters from C2 and DE groups (skilled and unskilled workers, casual workers, and the unemployed). American trends are now being repeated. Non-voters are more likely to identify as working class than middle class, less likely to own their house than rent a property, and less likely to have higher education qualifications. [27] There is a crisis of representation, and though it doesn't fall neatly along class or party lines, there are clearly discernible trends. These can be understood if we understand why the vote was struggled for in the first place, and what was done with it once obtained.

What is the point of voting?

Two economic historians at the Massachusetts Institute of Technology were faced with an historical puzzle. In the 19th Century, a series of sweeping political changes across Europe enfranchised previously unrepresented groups of people, mainly the adult male working class (women generally had to fight well into the twentieth century to obtain the franchise). The ruling classes in these societies had much to lose from conceding representative democracy to workers. Such changes tended to result in higher taxes on the rich, improved bargaining power for labour, a redistribution of wealth to the poor, and a reduction in inequality.

So why, given how much they stood to lose, did the rulers concede so much political power? Their analysis concluded that the rulers were forced to extend the franchise "because of the threat of revolution". "Extending the franchise," they contend, "is a commitment to future redistribution and prevents social unrest". The authors point out that the 1832 Reform Act, which was introduced by the ruling Whigs and enfranchised the emerging industrial capitalists, followed a period of unprecedented social upheaval and labour riots. Earl Grey, proposing the reforms, said: "The Principal of my reform is to prevent the necessity of revolution ... I am reforming to preserve, not to overthrow". And it was the perceived threat of revolutionary violence that put further enfranchisement on the agenda in 1867 – the Hyde Park riots of 1866, following the defeat of Gladstone's Reform Bill was the immediate stimulus for the Second Reform Act – and, again, in 1884.[28]

The emphasis on violence may be overstated. The Hyde Park riots, for example, were not particularly bloody, and the violence of counterrevolution has historically been much worse than that of revolution. However, the ruling class certainly had every reason to fear that, barring some concession of political power, they might lose their ability to rule. And the thesis has the advantage of reminding us that political power is above all concerned with the distribution of resources, and that the purpose of obtaining political power is to wield economic power (or, in the Marxist idiom, *class* power). It is also a rebuke to those genteel interpretations of British history, in which change is achieved through gradualist and pacific means. Before they would extend the franchise, the British ruling class had to be repeatedly placed in mortal terror, and even then it required five separate pieces of legislation over almost a century before it was fully won.

Even after the Third Reform Act in 1884, only about two thirds of adult males were able to vote, the vote was still tied to property and of course women were still excluded. Even so, it was a reform that frightened even some luminaries of the government that introduced it, because for the first time an electoral system that had been dominated by aristocrats, landowners and capitalists was now dominated – numerically at least - by working class voters. Just as senior Tories had feared the "disaster of democracy" they were courting in 1867, so William Harcourt, Gladstone's Home Secretary, described the 1884 Act as a "frightfully democratic measure which I confess appals me".[29] It was not until 1918, when the European continent was erupting with revolutionary energies inspired by

Russia, that the Fourth Reform Act enfranchised all adult males - and women for the first time, though they had to be rate-payers and over thirty. Even then, amendments forced through by the Conservative Party assured that the Tories would be over-represented.[30] Each advance for voting rights in Britain was foreshadowed by the prospect of existential peril for its rulers *as* rulers – something to think about.

What the working class – or the majority, about seventy percent, of the working class – then did with its vote was to support the Labour Party for almost a century. This was a party that was nominally committed to socialism after 1918, but also a party that was committed to parliamentarism. In practise, it delivered more of the latter than the former, but it was the primary electoral vehicle through which workers sought to realise their longer term goals and win some amelioration of their situation in the interim. Only the Communist Party came close to competing, and it had effectively conceded the monopoly of the socialist vote to Labour by the 1950s. This never meant that working class support for Labour was uncon-ditional, or could be taken for granted. The party's support collapsed in 1931 when, having governed as unemployment soared, cut public spending and reduced unemployment benefits, the Labour Prime Minister sacked his cabinet at the behest of the reactionary King George V and entered into a 'National Government' dominated by Tories and Liberals.[31]

Nor does it mean that joining or voting for Labour was the only form of political activity that workers engaged in. As Paul Mason has pointed out, before World War II, the British working class movement was characterised by vibrant cultures of syndi-calism, Marxism, anarchism and republicanism, in contrast to the quietest, respectability-seeking politics of the Parliamentary Labour Party.[32] However, Labour's subsequent ability to maintain the support of most working class voters rests princi-pally on the reputation it secured for delivering substantial reforms benefiting the working class in the post-war era. It says something about how powerful this reputation is that the historically anomalous era of social democracy is rather looked upon as a norm and the current neoliberal period as an aberration. Yet, despite the obvious advantages that working class people obtained from that settlement, its history tends to reinforce Ralph Miliband's argument that the role of democracy in a capitalist society is to contain pressure from below, and that the Labour Party functions as the chief means by which this takes place. His sons, Edward and David, both members of a Labour cabinet, surely grasp this. [33]

The limits of social democracy

The 'golden age'

The 1945 election was the first one in which the Labour Party won a majority, a popularity arising from the tremendous popular radicalisation that took place in Britain during World War II.[34] And it was the first Labour government which delivered on substantial parts of its programme. It is the object of nostalgia on the part of Labour supporters and parliamentarians alike, and its core achievement – the National Health Service – is universally defended. David Cameron even felt compelled, amid a torrent of American rightist vitriol toward Britain's socialist health service, to insist that the Tories were the "party of the NHS".[35] The NHS was just one of a series of socialising measures introduced by the government. The Bank of England was nationalised, the better to help the government implement Keynesian planning policies. Coal-mining was nationalised, and the old bosses replaced with the National Coal Board. Gas and electricity were nationalised. All nationalised industries were now formally accountable to a minister, and thus parliament. Thus, substantial parts of the economy were more democratic after Labour had finished than before.

Welfare was expanded with the National Assistance Act of

1948, finally replacing the last of the old Poor Laws, and the National Insurance Act of 1946, guaranteeing care for the elderly and benefits for all workers during periods of sickness and unemployment. National assistance was not set at a subsistence level as envisaged by Beveridge, but at a level relative to the average income, and was thus mildly redistributive, helping to reduce inequality.[36] Labour was rewarded for its reforms by working class electors, who kept the party in power in forty-two bye-elections. It lost the 1951 general election despite gaining the highest portion of the vote ever attained by a single party, some 48.8%, only because of the nature of the first-past-the-post system.[37] Even so, parliamentary democracy seemed to be working. The working class, having gained the franchise, had obtained sweeping reforms simply by voting for them. A third of Labour MPs brought to power in the landslide victory of 1945 were sponsored by trade unions, and thus there was an organic connection between the Parliamentary Labour Party and its working class base. The working class was at last represented in parliament. The Tories, meanwhile, did not dare reverse Labour's reforms. Instead, both main parties settled on a consensus colloquially known as 'Butskellism' after the Tory and Labour chancellors, Rab Butler and Hugh Gaitskell.

In general, the record of the social democratic era, roughly lasting from 1945 to 1975, would seem to be unsurpassed. Left-wing Keynesian economists Larry Elliott and Dan Atkinson point out that growth in that period exceeded that of the era since 1979, that employment was as close to being full in the post-war era as it ever had been under capitalism, and that incomes had a tendency to rise alongside productivity – pushed up by the collective strength of the working class in the trade union movement.[38] For working class people, the 'golden era' made a stable, planned future possible. It promised gradually rising living standards, more consumer durables, disposable income and leisure time. Above all, it would ensure that their children would have it easier than they themselves did.

The New Left

Yet, this being the case, there would appear to be a mystery as to why the first reaction against the post-war settlement, and the first signs of resistance, came from the New Left, not the New Right. If the first new Left emerged principally in response to the Soviet invasion of Hungary and Krushchev's revelations about the crimes of Stalin, the second New Left that arose in the Sixties had its sights aimed clearly at the post-war consensus. And why, if things were so rosy, did Labour governments so often find themselves having to renege on their commitments and engage in battles with their own supporters? Lastly, what made it possible for neoliberalism to emerge as a reaction against the consensus, with some basis in popular support?

To answer this, it is necessary to look afresh at the 'golden era'. There are perils in partaking of the maudlin sentimentality toward the Attlee government and the consensus it helped to establish. It was elected on a manifesto that declared Labour to be 'Socialist, and proud of it'. Yet it imitated its capitalist opponents in several important respects. For example, although Labour had nationalised important industries, it had never intended to go farther than creating a mixed economy. It nationalised a total of 20% of industry, and at that the main industries it nationalised were those which could not survive alone, and were necessary for sustainable capitalist development. As with the nationalisations of failing banks in the UK of late, the government was socialising *the costs of economic failure*, not the profits of industry.[39]

New Left socialists such as Ralph Miliband and Alasdair Macintyre argued that Labour's nationalisations, so far from being socialist in character, left capitalism intact. Labour had awarded "inconceivably generous" compensation to the owners of each industry nationalised, thus releasing funds that capital could re-invest in more profitable ways. It had paid for this with budget surpluses and public borrowing, thus diminishing the resources available to public services and making them less effective. It had not attempted, in its nationalisation programme, to redistribute power and wealth from the capitalist class to the majority. The nationalised industries were run on the basis of what was good for private industry, and the organisations set up to govern nationalised industries were 'public corporations' – hierarchical bodies based on the same worker-management relationship that obtained in private industry. In this respect, they retained a top-down, undemocratic structure, and their governing personnel tended to be drawn from the ranks of capital. Public services were also delivered in a high-handed, imperial fashion, modelled in part on the British experience of ruling India.[40]

Labour's manifesto commitment to nationalisation was always much more radical than anything the Labour leadership had intended to deliver. Over the objections of Labour's national executive, a young left-winger called Ian Mikardo had raised a motion at Labour's 1944 conference urging just such a commitment, and it was passed by delegates. As Ralph Miliband put it, what the Labour leadership wanted was "a continuation in peace time of the controls over economic life which had been introduced during the war, i.e. a more and better regulated peace-time *capitalist* economy". Even had Labour wanted to move in a socialist direction, its strategy for rebuilding a shattered economy came to depend on loans from the United States which, of course, came with binds. And it came to involve the suppression of strikes, using wartime legislation – the war against organised labour was to be a consistent theme of post-war Labour administrations, climaxing with *In Place of Strife*, through which legislation the Wilson government of 1966-1970 sought to curb the unions' right to strike, and the use of the army against striking firefighters.[41]

It was also the post-war Labour government which first locked the United Kingdom into its peculiar 'special relationship' with the American ruling class, imposed nuclear weapons on the country without even consulting the cabinet, supported Britain's entry into NATO, embroiled Britain in the Korean war, and sent the British Army to support right-wing monarchist and neo-fascist forces in Greece. Labour was, on questions of foreign policy, traditionally imperialist, violently suppressing anti-colonial movements, for example in Malaya. It also sent troops to assist the French restoration of colonial rule in Vietnam. One could go on, but the point is that Labour did not discover its imperial streak only when Tony Blair was elected.[42]

One theme that united the New Left's criticism of Labourism and the social democratic consensus was the latter's attitude to the capitalist state. Labour had seen the state as the means by which it would deliver, if not socialism, then at least capitalism with a human face. But it had never, even on its left-wing, taken a seriously critical look at the institution they were relying on. They believed that it was an autonomous social power that, once elected, they could control. But they were insufficiently attentive to just how consistently their policies had conformed to the existing distribution of wealth and power, how little in fact they had been able to substantially challenge the undemocratic concentrations of private economic power. Private capital had shown that it could act, through speculative attacks and other means, to subvert policies it did not like.

They also failed to acknowledge that, for example, the inter-penetration of the senior civil service with the managerial elite of private capital seriously undermined their ability to undertake reforms that would substantially alter the balance of wealth and power in favour of the working class. [43] This was a problem that Tony Benn encountered during his period as Secretary of State for Industry. Having persuaded Labour to seek office in 1974 on a far more radically democratic and redistributive agenda than in 1945, he found that the civil service were anxious to obstruct his reforms, particularly those involving creating cooperatives in some areas of industry, where workers would have a share of power and decision-making in those enterprises. Benn was supported in his case by Brian Sedgemore MP, who said that the civil service was "stuffed with reactionaries", and by the Labour national executive committee's Study Group which said it had an "in-built anti-socialist bias" and its neutrality was a myth.[44] Yet, though first-hand experience of the undemocratic nature of the state led many Labour MPs to see democratising the state as a primary political objective, the instrument they sought to use to do this was, well, the state.

The New Left could claim vindication as a result of this: the post-war consensus had absorbed some working class demands, and contained them. It had accepted some limited reforms, and stopped them going too far. If the purpose of gaining the vote was to wield economic power, Labour had wielded it mostly on behalf of the ruling class. It was, however, not the New Left's critique of post-war bureaucratism and statism that would prevail in the coming years. Working class radicalisation in the 1970s did provide opportunities for the Left, but it was mainly the Labour Left, not the extra-Labour Left, that grew as a result. As a consequence, the 1974-1979 Labour government's failure to deliver on its radical agenda, its spending cuts, its imposition of *de facto* wage cuts, and its prolonged, bitter wars with organised labour, simply demoralised the working class. This left it ripe for attack by an aggressive incoming Tory administration, which had its own critique of the state and of the post-war consensus.

The neoliberal revolt
Founding the neoliberal state
Neoliberalism has been construed as being mainly a set of economic policies. These involve the de-regulation of industry and finance, an emphasis on counter-inflation at the level of

macro-economic policy, and a growth model based on reduced labour costs. Unemployment could be countered but not through stimulus spending – rather, it was necessary to remove labour market 'rigidities' that inhibited hiring, by reducing employment protection for workers, union rights, taxes on business, and unemployment benefits. This policy mix in the UK was intended to restore profitability to British industry after a precipitous decline in the 1970s. The neoliberals around Thatcher had blamed 'special interests' embedded in the Keynesian state, especially trade unions, for tying down capital in inflexible and ossified organisational structures, thus holding back investment and growth. A dramatic shift in the balance of power between labour and capital, in favour of capital, was the indicated remedy – and the subsequent battles did help restore profitability somewhat, although investment remained low, productivity stagnated, and growth was never restored to its post-war peaks.[45]

However, it would be a mistake to see it in narrowly economic terms. Neoliberalism is also a political logic in which market values are extended into all forms of political and social action – everything from the civil service to healthcare delivery could be reformed along market lines. The arguments of 'public choice' theorists such as William Niskanen and James Buchanan were a crucial weapon in the neoliberals' intellectual armoury. They maintained that actors in the public sector behaved much like actors in the private sector – they were rationally self-interested. They acted on incentives to maximise their budgets, line their pockets, marginalise the public and pander to special interests. Therefore, public bureaucracies should be re-formed to behave as market actors. Internal markets could be introduced, on the assumption that competition would force bureaucracies to become more efficient. Spending caps could be introduced to disincentivise inefficiency and over-spend. Welfare should be reduced, since it incentivised state dependency – thus disincentivising employment and creating another special interest group. In general, the public sector should look more like the market. [46]

It is also important to recognise what is 'neo' about neoliberalism. Neoliberalism is not just classic laissez-faire economic liberalism. Neoliberalism may imply a model of 'human nature' as competitive and rationally self-interested. But in practise it does not assume that the behaviour it values is 'natural'. Rather, it sets out to institutionalise and incentivise the forms of behaviour that it sees as desirable. It does not simply interpret individuals as rational entrepreneurial actors, per *homo economicus*, but actively seeks to refashion individuals along those lines with a range of political and institutional reforms. [47]

Andrew Gamble notably anticipated the key developments of the Thatcher era, summarising her doctrine as tending toward a 'free economy' and a 'strong state'.[48] But this wasn't entirely right. The neoliberal policies Thatcher pioneered were highly interventionist in economic terms – policies that weakened organised labour, bailed out financial institutions, and depleted the manufacturing base were all forms of intervention that proved compatible with neoliberalism. This is why those on the Left who saw Brown's bail-outs of the banks as a departure from neoliberalism were gravely mistaken. Meanwhile, in its centralisation of political authority, it sought to *weaken* the state in its capacity as an actor independent of market forces. The Thatcherite attack on high-spending local councils, emblematised in its abolition of the Greater London Council, was not simply an attempt to strengthen the central state; it was an attempt to enforce market discipline in all areas of government. Cameron's embrace of localism, in this light, is not necessarily incompatible with his basic Thatcherite credentials. In the same way, George Osborne's pledge to 'free' public sector workers from the overbearing central state, by subordinating their work to market-driven targets, is an expression of Thatcherite ideology *par excellence.*

In subordinating statecraft at all levels to market rationality, and ultimately founding state legitimacy on its ability to generate economic growth, neoliberalism changed the character of the state. As such, the neoliberal project had profound implications for democracy. Neoliberal ideology is explicitly hostile to collective decision making, particularly those forms of collective decision making that are not mediated through the market. The idea that populations could vote for, say, high redistributive taxes and see that implemented is excluded by the founding tenets of the neoliberal state, which holds such practises to be harmful to economic growth and prosperity, and thus fatal to the legitimacy of the state.

Rolling back democracy
The Thatcherite counterrevolution was intellectually inspired by the writings of neoliberal ideologues such as the Austrian economist Friedrich von Hayek and Milton Friedman of the University of Chicago. Hayek was an appropriate *éminence grise* for the Thatcher administration. A student of Ludwig von Mises, he shared his mentor's grounding in classical liberalism and advocacy of 'pure' free market capitalism. Like his mentor, he abhorred infringements on the operations of capitalism, such as those that might be imposed by organised labour, or by parliamentary democracy. Mises admired Italian fascism for its defence of private property and thus for having saved European civilisation. "It cannot be denied," he wrote, "that Fascism and similar movements aiming at the establishment of dictatorships are full of the best intentions and that their intervention has, for the moment, saved European civilisation. The merit that Fascism has thereby won for itself will live on eternally in history."

When the dictatorship of Engelbert Dollfuss, modelled on its Italian parent, began to crush organised labour in 1934, Ludwig von Mises again approved. Mises and Dollfuss had co-written a

rites. They lie to opinion pollsters, telling them that they
...policies tending toward greater equality, socialisation of
...es and public services funded by higher taxes. But, they
...the Tories know our dark secret. Once in the privacy of the
...g booth, most of us will cast our votes for low taxes,
...tisation and inequality, on the selfish assumption that we
...t gain a little even if the poorest lose a lot. In fact, matters
...much simpler. People tell pollsters that they favour egali-
...n, collectivist measures because they in fact do favour these
...s, and they vote for them. The 'landslide' victories that the
...ervatives enjoyed in 1983 and 1987 were made possible by
...distorting influence of first-past-the-post, in which the
...ort of 42% of the electorate was translated as, respectively,
... and 58% of the available seats. An historian of the
...servative Party, Tim Bale, argues that: "Thatcher didn't win
...tions because she converted a majority of citizens to her
...e (she didn't) or because she was personally popular (she
...n't). She won them because her governments delivered just
...ugh tangible benefits to just enough voters at just the right
...es in order to defeat an opposition whose record in office was
...eful..."[53]

Some on the liberal-left respond to this by making an
...xceptionable case for constitutional reforms such as propor-
...al representation.[54] This makes sense – the factions of
...our split in the 1980s and are unlikely to be reunited in a
...gle organisation. But they have only needed each other for as
...g as there has been first-past-the-post. Proportional represen-
...ion could allow each party to represent their own base, while
...alescing in government to keep out the Tories; it would also
...e smaller parties a better chance of emerging. It would, of
...urse, involve Labour dropping its claim to a monopoly of all
...cial forces left-of-centre, but that goose is already cooked.

...However desirable electoral reform may be, though, the
...oblem is much more intractable than this solution would

report arguing that the causes of the Great Depression were not
market-driven but state-driven. Interventionist governments
had protected trade unions by keeping wages artificially high,
suppressed interest rates on borrowing, and taxed too much
property, thus limiting the production of capital. Thus, dictatorship in the interests of private property was a far more
suitable remedy to the problems of the Great Depression than
policies inspired by John Maynard Keynes or, worse, Karl Marx.
For Mises, as for the neoliberals inspired by him, fascism was an
appropriate "emergency makeshift" – but it was not a durable
system, nor ideal for preserving social relations based on private
property.[49]

Hayek, though he did not explicitly approve of interwar
fascism, was always conditional in his support for representative democracy. He viewed it as potentially a danger,
inasmuch as collective decision-making could over-ride
individual freedoms, specifically property rights. At best, it was
a means by which change might be made peaceably and
gradually, and the masses educated to an abhorrence of socialist
interventionism. But these were, as Perry Anderson notes,
"provisional and technical advantages" – democracy was not a
good in itself. Such was the wisdom that Margaret Thatcher
gleaned from *The Constitution of Liberty*.

Later, like Thatcher, and like the neoliberal group that he
inspired in Chicago, Hayek was an admirer of General Augusto
Pinochet. The Mont Pelerin society, which he co-founded, held
its meetings in Vina Del Mar, Chile, in 1981 as the dictatorship
was at its height. Interviewed by the pro-dictatorship
newspaper *El Mercurio*, Hayek stated, "Personally I prefer a
liberal dictator to democratic government lacking liberalism."
The 'Chicago Boys', a school of economists based at the
University of Chicago who were inspired by Hayek, Mises and
Milton Friedman, gained considerable influence in Pinochet's
Chile, recommending anti-inflationary measures, deep cuts to

state expenditure, and the privatisation of public assets such as pensions and healthcare. Their support for Pinochet, like Mises' support for Italian fascism, was based on their view that it was a necessary 'transitional' arrangement, reversing democratic interference in the economy and restoring the grounds for individual liberty.[50]

Thatcher, though sharing his ends, acknowledged that it would not appropriate to import the dictator's methods to the United Kingdom. She would have to create a consensus. However, to do that, it was necessary to plan for all-out war against those considerable segments of the population that were well-placed to resist her policies, particularly organised labour. This involved her in a series of carefully chosen set-piece battles, outlined first in the 'Ridley Plan'. The plan was drawn up in response to the 1974 miners' strike, the second such to defeat the Heath administration, and the one which led to Heath declaring a general election, asking the electorate who should run the country – he or the miners. Heath lost. The Thatcherites, operating both in the Conservative Party and in an array of think-tanks where Hayekian ideology was propagated, such as the Institute of Economic Affairs, were determined never to allow this to happen again. Managers should have the right to manage, businesses the right to invest, and states the right to govern.

So, Nicholas Ridley drew up a plan to reform the public sector, privatising much of it, abolishing statutory monopolies, and strengthening management. Wage settlements would no longer be determined by comparison to equivalent wages in other industries. Rather, the deciding factor would be the strength of the workers with respect to management, as determined by the supply of workers and their relative capacity for effective strike action. This was a signal that workers could no longer depend on collective bargaining to obtain wage improvements – they would have to fight for it.

In an annexe to his report, Ridley o[...] needed to overcome political oppositio[...] Workers suffering redundancies or depress[...] to be at the forefront of this opposition. Th[...] to fight the war in stages. Industries that [...] strikes should be given higher than avera[...] thus preventing them from entering into th[...] should choose their first battle in an industr[...] were weak and where they were confider[...] should reduce benefit payments to the wives[...] strikers. And in the meantime, prepar[...] confrontation with the mineworkers, they sh[...] stocks, recruit non-union drivers and build u[...] mobile police squad to break pickets and all[...] drivers to enter work sites.[51]

In order to defeat the miners, a wide-rangin[...] tions was set in motion, including the use of[...] teurs, forgeries and surveillance by Special [...] Nigel Lawson, who had been Energy Secre[...] planning for the miners' strike, recalled that it [...] arming to face the threat of Hitler in the 1930s"[...] revelations have made clear, the aim was not me[...] and defeat strikes so that the neoliberal progr[...] carried through. It was to destroy the social ba[...] militant and powerful trade union in Britain. T[...] was to be confirmed just as New Labour emerge[...] Labour chrysalis, with the privatisation in 199[...] industry, the single most important asset natio[...] Attlee administration.[52] But the defeat of organis[...] only one component of achieving the consens[...] neoliberalism.

Constructing a new consensus: from the SDP to New L[...]
It is a commonplace of the political right that mo[...]

suggest. If it is true that most people have consistently voted against the policies imposed by the Thatcherite wing of the Conservative Party, this is also true of voters on the continent where similar policies were introduced. For example, the Mitterrand government in France was elected in 1981 on an agenda of far-reaching social democratic reform. With the assistance of right-ward moving intellectuals such as Francois Furet and Bernard-Henri Levy who resisted leftist temptations within the Socialist Party, capital effectively sank the reform agenda and forced a deflationary programme of fiscal austerity and financialisation on the government. Voters "unfailingly rejected every government" that tried to administer the neoliberal medicine, but each successive government nonetheless consistently force-fed it to the electorate.[55] Neoliberalism has been imposed by political and economic elites in most advanced capitalist states regardless of the voting arrangements in those polities. And this is indeed what we would expect if the New Left critique of the capitalist state is valid.

However, it is important to see that Thatcher couldn't just impose neoliberalism: she had to fight to win people over to the neoliberal vision. Partly this was helped by the radical reconstitution of the UK's social fabric, which created a constituency that would be vested in the neoliberal settlement. In this respect, Tory policy fundamentally recomposed the working class by sinking the manufacturing sector and moving toward a service-based economy, running down council housing and promoting home ownership, promoting private debt and financialising the economy.

The destruction of manufacturing saw manufacturing employment fall by 30% in the UK between 1979 and 1990. This slash-and-burn represented a faster rate of de-industrialisation than in comparable European economies. Union membership fell by almost a half. As a side effect, it also hollowed out many of the social bases from which the Left drew its strength and in which cultures of resistance were maintained. By rationing housing, the government helped send house prices soaring. After 1983, the Tories imposed a moratorium on public housing, with the rate of annual construction falling from 160,000 in 1975 to 25,000 in 1990. The level of housing expenditure fell from 1.4% of GDP in 1979 to 0.4% in 1990. And owner occupation increased in the same period from 60% to 72%. Homeowners were encouraged to treat their houses as assets against which they could borrow, to pay for the consumer durables that stagnant wages no longer would. There was also a conspicuous effort to persuade people to buy shares, particularly in privatised enterprises such as British Gas – this was less successful. Individual share ownership never made a big impression on the stock market, and it was at an all-time low in 2010.[56]

Still, even if high unemployment became a permanent fixture of the social setting, poverty rose from 1% of the population to almost a quarter, and homelessness re-emerged as a major social problem, there was a layer of the population that would feel wealthy enough to vote for Margaret Thatcher, and that did not have to be a majority. As Luc Boltanski and Eve Chiapello point out, the new phase of capitalism also required a new 'spirit of capitalism' as it were. This entailed a cultural war to persuade people – not the majority, but a sufficient minority, and particularly the middle classes who would have managerial or supervisorial roles – that what they wanted above all was not the safety nets and security of the post-war era, but the flexibility, risk and protean adventure of free market competition.[57] In this way, with some people economically vested in neoliberalism and others ideologically committed to defending it and expanding its dominion, a hegemonic regime could be constructed.

By far more important, perhaps, was the success in forcing the Labour Party to adapt to neoliberalism and thus to the radical contraction in democratic possibilities that it entailed. I discuss some of the consequences in more detail in Chapter Two, but let us outline some of the contours of this transition. First of all, the emergence of a large centre vote in the 1980s seemed to many Labour activists to signal a fundamental shift in the electorate.

The vote for the Liberal/Social Democratic Party Alliance in 1983 was the biggest vote for a third party since the 1920s. Labour's vote was the lowest since 1918. On top of this, only 39% of trade union members voted Labour in 1983. Of all manual working class voters, only half voted for Labour, 20% for the Liberal/SDP Alliance and 30% for the Tories. In 1987, the Alliance won almost 23% of the vote, and 60% of trade unionists voted for parties other than Labour. It is important not to overstate this: class remained a powerful factor in UK political alignment. Even at Labour's lowest point in 1983, manual workers were the least likely to vote Tory and the most likely to vote Labour, while the Tory bedrock was the petit-bourgeoisie, 70% of whom voted for Thatcher. But even so, the split in the working class vote was the single biggest reason for the Tory victories in the 1980s.[58]

It was one thing to attack the defection of the 'gang of four', those senior Labour MPs who reneged on their party and consciously sought to realign British politics toward the centre. It is true that through their actions, they helped Thatcher to remain in power. But there was a real question of why millions of workers voted for them. Some argued that the 'forward march of Labour' had been halted. Seventies militancy had not been based on a real improvement in the strength of the working class, and thus was vulnerable to sudden downturns and right-ward shifts.

The Labour leadership, supported by intellectuals in the Communist Party such as Eric Hobsbawm, argued for a move to the right in order to construct a wider electoral front against Thatcherism. There were many social forces both inside the working class and the professional middle classes who would not vote for a radical left-wing programme, but who would rally behind a moderate centre-left agenda. The Bennites had to be defeated; Militant had to be rooted out; the moderate leadership of Neil Kinnock and Roy Hattersley had to be supported. Later, especially after the bruising defeat Labour suffered in 1987, they argued that British society was entering 'New Times', demanding that the left accept pro-market (read neoliberal) policies if it was to win back middle class voters. And Neil Kinnock seemed to be doing that. He was restoring the coalition between workers and the progressive middle class, just as Thatcher was shredding Tory support with the Poll Tax. So the 1992 election defeat was, for Labour members and supporters of this persuasion, utterly inexplicable and utterly demoralising. When John Smith died and Tony Blair and his allies took control of the Labour Party, they found an organisation that could put up little resistance to their right-wing agenda.[59]

There is a conundrum here. The Labour Right probably represented most of the party's membership since 1981 when a right-wing majority gained control of the NEC for the first time in a decade. The influence of Bennism in the early 1980s, though genuinely enthusing a minority of the party, was exaggerated by union block votes. The witch-hunts against Militant proved, not that the Left was powerful, but that it was weak.[60] Labour's right-wing faced few difficulties in imposing the policies and objectives that it thought would win elections, yet it consistently failed to do so. Peter Mandelson and Philip Gould, co-architects of New Labour, were also architects of Labour's failed election strategies in 1987 and 1992. Only with the complete enervation of the Tories, and the abdication of social democracy on Labour's part, did the goal of uniting core working class Labour supporters with middle class voters to produce an electoral plurality actually materialise. But at that point a broomstick with a red rosette could plausibly have stood against John Major and won.

To add to the conundrum, as mentioned above, the hard right leadership of Tony Blair and Gordon Brown only managed to secure three successive election victories because of the miserable state of the Conservative Party. Labour's electoral coalition has consistently contracted since 1997, such that its victories in 2001 and 2005 were based on poorer votes than Labour obtained in 1992. So, if the correct strategy was to abandon any suspicion of left-wing politics, agree vigorously with Margaret Thatcher that the old class divisions no longer applied, and enthusiastically adopt Conservative policies, why didn't it work? Evidently, it was never the correct strategy. Voter who abandoned Labour for the Alliance were not uncomplicatedly centrist, and they were certainly not won over to the Thatcherite agenda. On social issues such as immigration, defence and crime, they were left-wing; on economic issues, they were centrist, but not Thatcherite.[61]

If Labour was aiming to add these votes to its core electorate, then its embrace of Thatcherism, not only in the economy but also on immigration and defence, was wholly self-defeating. It has placed the party to the right of the public on a series of defining policy issues, not least privatisation and war. However, it was also wholly consistent with the neoliberal order which, we have mentioned, has ramifications not only for the economy, but also the polity – even on 'social' issues such as crime and punishment, and immigration, wherein tougher sentences on the one hand and state-sanctioned poverty on the other are (wrongly) assumed to form part of the incentive structure to discourage rational-economic actors from engaging in behaviour that the state wishes to prohibit.[62]

I would hypothesise that what happened to Labour was less an adjustment to psephological realities than an adjustment to socioeconomic realities. The Tories' defeat of one union after another confirmed that capital's power with respect to labour had increased, and that realistically it could also defeat any government that did not implement the fiscal, financial, and macroeconomic reforms that it supported, and which had been carefully elaborated in business-funded think-tanks as well as in the terror-state laboratories of Latin America. Labour thus set out to prove its credentials to businesses and the right-wing media, showing that it accepted every tenet of neoliberal doctrine even at the expense of offending or losing core voters. This culminated in New Labour's grubby relationship with Rupert Murdoch, and Tony Blair's crawling before the rich.

The obvious answer to this dilemma, which leaves us with three parties each committed to neoliberalism and the social interests it serves, is to try to strengthen the position of the working class with respect to capital. But this is a long game, and it is not the sort of thing the Labour Party does. Labour's parliamentarism means that it expects its supporters to be passive, that it never tries to arouse them to protest or militancy and that, quite often where militancy does erupt, Labour is on the opposing side (as happened with the Poll Tax riots). That essentially passive, top-down conception of political activity has been one of the problems with Labourism from its inception, and one of the reasons why it has so often failed in its objective of giving political representation to the working class, and why the promise of the franchise has never really been fulfilled.

Conclusion: the trouble with passivity

The paradox of the vote is that it was one right that assuredly could not be achieved by voting for it. In the same way, reforms gained from parliament were usually not achieved by exclusively reformist means. Popular pressure has had to be applied. The mass antiwar protests in 2003 showed just how much pressure it can take to force a change of policy: apparently, two million people on the streets just doesn't cut it these days. Politicians promise to 'restore trust' in themselves and in the institutions they work in – well, they would, wouldn't they?

They promise to democratise the system, to invite people – as the Tories say on the cover of their 2010 manifesto – to "partic- ipate in the government of the United Kingdom". If we fall for this, as some might, it is because we have forgotten that the most basic democracy, as well as more radical democratic gains, had to be fought for.

I have argued that the real democratic deficit arises from the fact that working class people, who constitute the vast majority of society contrary to endless back-slapping editorials about what a fabulously open and meritocratic society we have, are not being represented. I don't simply mean that there isn't enough difference between the major parties. The larger parties have *always* tended to converge toward a similar programme – such is the domesticating effect that parliament has on its inhab- itants. I mean that the neoliberal state has less and less capacity to register their interests. I also mean that the institutional bases through which the working class could force parliament to absorb its demands are less and less effective in doing so.

Trade unions represent less than a third of British workers, and lack the clout they would need to force more than a few meagre reforms onto the table. More than that, their leaders are – as PCS general secretary Mark Serwotka has complained – all too often more loyal to the leadership of the Parliamentary Labour Party than they are to their own members. The Labour Party is internally more undemocratic than it has ever been, it is dominated by a clique of hard right free marketers, and its membership is now disproportionately middle class anyway. As for the Tories – well, the Tories like the workers. Someone has to build their duck islands for them. But they are the party of capital, and they have resisted every effort by the working class to have its say, from the franchise onward. In a less gentrified age, we would have said they were our 'class enemies'.

Now, in the final stages of the 2010 election, we hear that many former Labour voters might switch to the Liberal

Democrats and their glamorous young leader, Nick Clegg. We hear from pundits that it is now possible to have a 'Cleggasm', though I suspect that anti-climax is a far more likely outcome. Should the Liberal Democrats succeed in taking some of the left-of-centre votes from New Labour, however, it will only consolidate the very political project that the Blairites initiated: to drop the whole idea of the working class having independent interests and an independent political party, and merge Labourism with Liberalism. We urgently need real representation.

The scattered forces of the Left have tried to come up with various new parties and coalitions to offer just that. In 2010, we have a variety of left-wing campaigns based on the idea of representing working class people, among which the most likely candidates are the Trade Unionists and Socialist Coalition (TUSC), and Respect. But though successes for them would be a step forward, they are building from the margins, with few resources, and their gains are likely to be highly localised (though one has to fancy the chances of Salma Yaqoob, Respect's candidate in Birmingham). In truth, it is only through working class people organising themselves, whether it is unionising their workplaces, or setting up community organisations, or forming coalitions urgently to stop the savage public spending cuts that await us, and the jobs massacres that will come with it, that they will come up with new ways to ensure that they are represented politically. If non-voting is problematic, political passivity is suicide.

Chapter Two

'Meritocracy'

David Cameron describes himself as a meritocrat with the plati-tudinous confidence of someone describing herself as a believer in free elections. So do his opponents. Gordon Brown has pledged in this election, yet again, to fight for a "genuine meritocracy" based on a skilled economy.[63] Everyone, seemingly, is a meritocrat. The word has become synonymous with a belief in fairness: that one should rise or fall by one's own merits is as close to a common sense idea as any. It was not always so. Meritocracy was once a revolutionary idea. The French revolutionaries demanded *"la carrière ouverte aux talents"* ("careers open to the talents"), as Napoleon's maxim had it, against the aristocratic order in which opportunities were reserved for those of noble birth.[64] For Thomas Paine, the principle of monarchy could be indicted in large part because it meant the rule of the least capable.[65] For Thomas Jefferson, the American revolution had succeeded in creating an "aristocracy of talent".[66] From being the credo of revolutionaries, meritocracy has become an axiom of liberal capitalism, so apparently self-evident that only the wicked or perverse would oppose it.

Yet meritocracy, as a doctrine of hierarchy, also contradicts a founding tenet of the 18th Century revolutionary legacy, that of equality. It appeals to a desire, which John Adams detected in Americans, for distinction in relation to one's peers. This sense of mastery over others has long been manipulated by the right to accommodate even some of the poorest to their lot.[67] The language of meritocracy is, or so I will argue, a language of class rule. I would also propose that the term, as applied to the present state of affairs, is a kind of collective insult on humankind. To imply that those currently at the top – the Warren Buffets and Roman Abramoviches of this world – are the very best, the *nec plus ultra* of humanity, is a kind of hate speech toward the species. Dignity demands that we refute it.

Conservatism and the ideology of excellence
Thatcherites-in-drag
David Cameron has undertaken to promote a "brazen elitism" in education, betokened thus far by a promise to prevent students with a third class degree from training to become teachers. Perhaps less important than the policy – which suddenly appeared as foolish as it was arbitrary when it transpired that their "mathematics czar", Carole Vorderman, was in possession of a third class degree – is the broader intention signalled by the policy.[68] The Tories have of late evinced an antipathy to the widening gap between the rich and the poor. David Cameron has cited research by Richard Wilkinson and Kate Pickett, demonstrating that societies with high levels of inequality suffer acute social distress as a result of it.[69] But, like New Labour, the Tories would rather 'level up' than 'level down'. By improving the quality of teachers, they maintain, they can equalise opportunities for the poor, allowing more of them compete on more equal terms with their wealthier counterparts, and succeed.

So also with their policies aimed at attacking family failure and single parenthood. David Cameron has claimed that class background is statistically insignificant in determining life chances provided the child has a stable two-parent family. To promote the cause of equality, 'therefore the state must encourage poor people to buck up and live right. Thus, the Tories will insist on imposing tax changes that, however nugatory, signal an endorsement of marriage and a disapprobation of single parent families.[70] This is Lilliputian economics. A benefit worth less than £3 a week would make little difference to people's life choices. The real solvent of families is economic distress – the Tories might be expected to understand that their war on the idea of a 'job for life' would inevitably result in the end of a 'family for life'.

However, the means – 'levelling up' – implies a diagnosis, which is that inequality arises not because the rich accumulate too much of the wealth produced by society, but because the poor fail to excel. They are 'socially excluded', rather than exploited. Discourses of 'social exclusion' suggest that the problem of inequality arises because, for example, parents lack child-rearing skills and moral fibre, not because the dynamics of the capitalist economy have tended to accelerate the unequal distribution of wealth for some thirty years. [71] It also implies an end, which is not equality – so far from it - but inequality of a particular character. It implies a meritocracy, in short, in which achievement is correlated to ability rather than class background. In this, though dragging up as social workers and charity do-gooders, and though availing themselves of territory prepared by New Labour, the Conservatives are remaining true and blue. Their aim, belying the pseudo-egalitarian rhetoric, is to moralise the class system, to ensure that privilege is seen as co-substantial with achievement, financial success with excellence.

Excellence and the conservative tradition

It is a mainstay of conservative political philosophy that there is a contradiction between excellence and equality. Burke, the founder of modern conservatism, objected to egalitarianism on the grounds that inequality of conditions grew not out of exploitation and oppression, but from "the nature of things", and was the result of the "accumulation, permutation and improvement of property". This inequality, he vouched, was nearer the "true equality" of human beings, which was an equality of souls in the eyes of the Almighty. Inequality, that is to say, represented the proper flourishing of humanity, and attempts to overthrow it would at best stifle that flourishing, at worst lead to mob rule and anarchy. Such attempts, moreover, were motivated by nothing more than the politics of envy – it was the place of the lower orders to accept their naturally subordinate position, for without a "natural aristocracy", there was no nation and no civilisation.[72]

This is an idea that runs throughout conservative thought. Alexis de Tocqueville's fear when observing the outcome of the American revolution was that the equality of citizens in making the law could undermine excellence in its formulation and application. [73] In Friedrich Nietzsche's various attacks on socialism and democracy, what disgusts him most is the idea of mediocrity, the spectre of the "last man". The best ages of mankind are characterised, he maintains, by a "pathos of distance" between the ruling order and the lower classes, which is responsible for "every enhancement of the type 'man'". [74]

Friedrich von Hayek's critique of planned economies was, among other things, founded on the belief that it would stifle human creativity. A leisure class was necessary to produce cultural excellence. Any attempt to relieve the wealthy of their riches would only ensure that similar wealth not be reproduced, and that the cultural progress and dynamism that they alone could produce would be lost.[75] For Ayn Rand, the conditions that would produce equality would also produce a conformist tyranny. In Rand's *The Fountainhead*, the maleficent antagonist and would-be dictator Ellsworth Toohey – a composite of Harold Laski and Joseph Stalin – outlines the essence of his egalitarian plot: "Let progress stop. Let all stagnate. There's equality in stagnation. All subjugated to the will of all ..." To bring about this dystopia, he must extinguish all aspiration, all ability to recognise greatness and achieve it, as "great men can't be ruled".[76]

In general, the conservative critique of egalitarianism, and the defence of every hierarchy from plantation slavery to wage slavery, is marked by just this evocation of stagnation. [77] This is one reason why conservatives champion the language, if not the practise, of liberty. It may seem inapposite since, historically, conservatives have maintained that authority and coercion was necessary to force the majority to be productive. Such was the case of American slavers, for example. But coercion under capitalism principally works to defend the boundaries of established economic relations rather than intervening in daily production. Economic coercion, the threat of being without, is dominant. So, conservatives prefer to rely on the incentive of inequality to drive people to produce.[78] Thus, maintaining that in conditions of liberty (from taxes and regulations, chiefly) there will always arise a natural hierarchy, conservatives hold that equality is the ignoble and selfish goal of envious inferiors. That was the meaning of the statement, by the President of Yale in 1925, that equality was the ideal of lesser races and freedom the ideal of superior races.[79] This is what the freedom to be unequal is, in the last analysis, reducible to.

An insight from Karl Mannheim's essay on "The Democratisation of Culture" suggests that this 'heroic' individualism might have a particular class basis. He notes that for those who have achieved status as a result of (what appears to be) individual achievement – they might today be said to be the *nouveaux riches* and petit-bourgeois that Thatcher championed – cultural excellence and civilisation appear to result from discontinuous moments of inspiration and creation, rather than the cumulative result of a cooperative effort.[80] Meritocracy, then, would be most appealing as an ideal to those whose social position leads them to see their own successes, however minor, as the result of their exclusive efforts and genius.

Thatcher and the meritocracy
The invention of the term 'meritocracy' owes itself to the sociol-

ogist Michael Young, a Labour Party activist who had drafted the manifesto that saw Labour elected in 1945. In 1958, he wrote a sociological fantasy, *The Rise of the Meritocracy*, in which the ascendancy of a privileged elite is described, its origins traced from 1870, when education was made compulsory in the UK and patronage in the civil service abolished. The education system produced a population graded not by rank but by certificate, and the civil service model of competitive entry was successfully replicated in thousands of private enterprise. The denouement, set in 2033, has seen a new elite emerge based on intelligence testing and educational selection.[81] The book, declined for publication by the Fabian Society, was a warning to Labour that the acceptance of 'merit' as the basis for inequality could merely reinvent the class system. The later uses of his neologism dismayed the author, and missed the point.

Two years after Young's satire was published, the Austrian free market economist Friedrich Hayek wrote *The Constitution of Liberty*. The accumulation of wealth and privilege held no terror for Hayek – it was natural, and it brought with it social and cultural advantages that would be lost if it were suppressed. This was a founding text for the New Right and the bible of the Thatcherites. As leader of the opposition in the late 1970s, Margaret Thatcher is reputed to have faced down centrist critics by raising a copy of the text for all to see. "This," she said, "is what we believe." And she banged the book on the table. Hayek was also prominent in supporting the Conservatives' election in 1979 and its campaign against the trade unions. [82] But although Thatcher owed much to Hayek philosophically, her grounds for rejecting equality differed slightly.

Hayek did not approve of basing the case for free markets and individual sovereignty on an appeal to merit. In *The Constitution of Liberty*, he argued that "[Neither] those differences in individual capacities which are inborn [nor] those which are due to the influences of environment ... has anything to do with moral merit. Though either may greatly affect the value which an individual has for his fellows, no more credit belongs to him for having been born with desirable qualities than for having grown up under favourable circumstances." This is an argument which, interestingly, he shared with the egalitarian liberal John Rawls.[83]

By the time Margaret Thatcher had become the leader of the Conservative Party, 'meritocracy' had entered political discourse and acquired connotations quite contrary to those intended by its author. The language of merit based on individual abilities turned out to be an attractive way to code an appeal for inequality. This was expressed in Thatcher's 1975 speech, "Let Our Children Grow Tall", rejecting the Butskellite consensus that had under-written the post-war order:

> Now, what are the lessons then that we've learned from the last thirty years? First, that the pursuit of equality itself is a mirage. What's more desirable and more practicable than the pursuit of equality is the pursuit of equality of opportunity. And opportunity means nothing unless it includes the right to be unequal and the freedom to be different. One of the reasons that we value individuals is not because they're all the same, but because they're all different. I believe you have a saying in the Middle West: "Don't cut down the tall poppies. Let them rather grow tall." I would say, let our children grow tall and some taller than others if they have the ability in them to do so. Because we must build a society in which each citizen can develop his full potential, both for his own benefit and for the community as a whole, a society in which originality, skill, energy and thrift are rewarded, in which we encourage rather than restrict the variety and richness of human nature.[84]

Here, we have the meritocratic creed in all of its glamour and tawdriness. Continuous with Burke, Thatcher sees hierarchy as an appropriate kind of *diversity*, and in line with past conservative thought sees privilege as an expression of freedom and human flourishing. Again, moving a declaration of 'no confidence' in the decrepit Callaghan government, as leader of the Opposition in 1977, Thatcher again cited the inadequacy of egalitarianism next to meritocracy:

> Perhaps one of the reasons why so many of our constituents have left support of the Socialist Government was put very well in an article called "Maligning Merit" in The Sunday Telegraph Magazine a few weeks ago by Mrs. J. B. Priestley, the author Jacquetta Hawkes, when she said: "for me Labour showed that it had gone astray when it used meritocracy as a dirty word. My utter conviction that egalitarianism is wrong in theory and positively evil in practice has grown mainly from observing what is being done in its name today." Her views are shared by many people.[85]

Defending her decision to keep grammar schools in 1983, she said they were necessary institutions to allow "people like me" to climb the ladder – though in fact, Thatcher's most rapid moment of upward social mobility was her wedding day, when she married into the oil business and was wealthy ever after. "I believe in merit," she nevertheless explained. "I belong to meritocracy, and I don't care two hoots what your background is. What I am concerned with is whatever your background, you have a chance to climb to the top".[86]

I don't claim that Thatcher's policies actually achieved a meritocracy, or sought to, supposing such a chimera to be actually possible. But, as Chapter One describes, she did preside over a social landscape increasingly marked by permanently high rates of unemployment, growing inequality and social distress. The zenith of her era was characterised by the flamboyant consumption of those who became rich out of privatisation, the deregulation of the stock market and the soaring cost of real estate.

Meritocracy was one vital ideological tool in the Tories' war on the idea of equality. It provided the Tories with a superficially attractive weapon with which to openly and proudly attack such ideals, to reconcile people to the meaner and less secure environment produced by their policies, and encourage them to pursue individual, entrepreneurial solutions to their problems rather than collective, socialist or trade union-based alternatives. And it assured those who had made what is colloquially known as a 'killing' out of the mass misery that resulted that their rewards were deserved. It was perhaps ironic, then, that Thatcher's political opponents not only embraced the ideology of merit, but took it far more seriously than she herself did.

New Labour and meritocracy
The terminus of class war
New Labour first moved to embrace the goal of meritocracy through the work of the Commission on Social Justice. The Commission's report asserted, contra John Rawls and Friedrich Hayek, that the more talented are in some sense deserving of their talents, and therefore deserving of greater rewards. From then on, it became central to Third Way thinking about welfare and social justice. In practical terms, this meant – aside from the Blairites' war on Labour's exhausted and shattered Left, and the erasure of 'clause four' from Labour's constitution – abandoning redistribution of wealth as a goal, which could be seen as capping 'achievement', and instead seeking to reform the tax and benefits system to incentivise work and reduce the worst forms of poverty, especially child poverty. It meant "a hand up, not a hand out" for the 20% of households without a single earner. It meant the introduction of a minimum wage and the

creation of a social exclusion unit. In short, the government would rectify the extremes of poverty and disadvantage that were held to prevent people from engaging in the meritocratic competition, but would not attempt to create a more equal society.[87]

In ideological terms, the embrace of meritocracy meant declaring – *pace* Blair – that the class war was over. This was not a view shared by the public which had, a year before Blair's election, been polled on this very issue: 81% of people believed that there was a class war going on in the UK.[88] But then, contrary to the image of Blair as a consensual politician guided overly by public opinion, he was a doctrinal thinker who was quite prepared to fight his party and his electorate over key issues, and move the agenda to the right – not only on class, but also on privatisation, and war. John Prescott agreed with Tony Blair, asserting that "we're all middle class now". To prove the government's case, the Office for National Statistics even produced a new set of classifications according to which we were indeed all, or mostly, middle class – though a majority still self-identify as working class.[89]

Not only was the ideology of meritocracy essential to New Labour's approach to social justice. It was also part of their growth strategy, and consequently their strategy for funding public services and meliorist reforms. Stephen Byers, representing the ultra-Blairites in New Labour, declaimed that wealth creation was more important than the redistribution of wealth. Rather than a more equal society, he said, New Labour should aim to create a business climate in which the wealth-creators could thrive. This would fund public services, and create the revenues to help tackle "social exclusion".[90] Thus, rather than raising taxes on high income earners, corporations and personal wealth, the government froze income taxes on the highest earners, cut corporation taxes and small business taxes, and tried to make the regulatory environment as exiguous as possible.

A nastier side of this has been the moralism, bullying and social authoritarianism that the government promulgated in the course of its battle with 'social exclusion'. Thus, in one of its headline-friendly initiatives regarding educational exclusion, it threatened the parents of truant children with increased fines. This was a cheap and easy solution that failed to address the multitude of social problems that create truancy, identifying the most important problem as parents who lack moral fibre.[91] Street curfews, ASBOs, the proliferation of CCTV and the proposal for pre-emptive intervention in potential problem families with surveillance before the child has said her first word, are all part of the same package. This follows from New Labour's approach to 'social exclusion', which is held to be caused in large part by the dysfunctional behaviour of a significant minority of working class people.[92]

At the zenith of Blairite rule, some challenges to this consensus on 'meritocracy' emerged. Stephen Aldridge of the Cabinet Office's Performance and Innovation Unit composed a report on how meritocracy could be achieved in Britain. He was not aiming for controversy, but his conclusions – delivered to a host of Third Way intellectuals such as Anthony Giddens and Geoff Mulgan – scandalised his bosses. He said that to have a 'strong' version of meritocracy, it would be necessary to raise taxes on income and investments, and abolish inheritance. For social mobility to realistically take place, it had to be possible to move down as well as up the scale, and thus it would be necessary to "reduce barriers to downward social mobility for dull middle class children". [93] The government distanced itself from these findings – this was not the meritocracy they had in mind.

Michael Young also inconveniently emerged to dispute Labour's endorsement of meritocracy. Merit, he pointed out, was not class-neutral. The education system had worked to concentrate the attributes constituting merit among the privileged, doing down the poor and disadvantaged. Meanwhile, since the rich were encouraged to believe that their privileges were earned, resulting from proven merit, they had come to believe that they were entitled to whatever they could lay their hands on. Inequality had soared, as the "insufferably smug" new elite grabbed higher salaries, more share options, larger bonuses and more generous 'golden handshakes'. He urged Blair to disassociate his government from the language of 'meritocracy' and tax the income of the rich, the better to support advancement for the poor.[94] As in 1958, though, his efforts were to be in vain.

Those magnificent wealth creators

An obnoxious counterpart to all of this was New Labour's unabashed, unashamed, emetic crawling to the rich. For, if Britain was a meritocracy, some unfortunate social exclusion notwithstanding, it followed that its rich were extraordinary people – achievers, risk-takers, 'wealth creators'. Accordingly New Labour began to extol the virtues of those 'wealth creators', lavishly serenading the richest businessmen, offering them patronage and cabinet posts (they must know how to run things after all), throwing knighthoods at them, and holding them up as models for others to emulate.

Many New Labour ministers, when no longer in ministerial posts, decided they liked the rich so much that they had to be around them as much as possible. So they departed for lucrative careers, for example in the private finance industry that they had done so much to cultivate. And they themselves must be very special people. In the run up to the 2010 election campaign, three former New Labour cabinet ministers – Stephen Byers, Patricia Hewitt and Geoff Hoon – were caught on camera in a Channel 4 sting operation telling what they believed was a representative of an American lobbying company that they were for hire and could change government policy if paid £5,000 a day to do so.

Setting aside the promise to subvert democracy for a second, the fee discussed here was actually more than one of their unemployed constituents would receive in Job Seekers Allowance in a whole year. In the arithmetic of meritocracy, this means that Geoff Hoon is worth more than 500 of his unemployed constituents.

An alternative perspective is provided by the New Economics Foundation which reported in December 2009 that hospital cleaners and child minders added more to society's wealth than the far more highly remunerated bankers and advertisers. While a childcare worker created, on average, £9.50 for every pound she was paid, a City banker would manage to *destroy* £7 for every £1 earned. The irony of calling such people 'wealth creators' is hard to miss.[95]

Inequality rising

It has been argued by the Institute of Fiscal Studies that the overall impact of New Labour's tax policies was in fact, if not in explicit intent, redistributive. Yet, the same institution also found that under New Labour, inequality had soared to the highest levels since records began.[96] So, what gives? Simply that New Labour's moderate forms of stealth redistribution were outweighed by the impact of their other policies. As noted in Chapter One, New Labour maintained the very features of British economic life that had produced such dramatic increases in inequality since 1979.

We have seen that New Labour identified its key social problem as the 'socially excluded' 'underclass' – the fifth of households with no one in employment. Gordon Brown therefore sought to reduce unemployment. But he also explicitly endorsed neoliberal economics, including Milton Friedman's resuscitation of the idea of a 'natural rate of unemployment', or 'non-accelerating inflation rate of unemployment' (NAIRU) in contemporary parlance. According to this dogma, any attempt to reduce unemployment below a certain level through Keynesian demand management would simply result in soaring inflation. He also endorsed Tory chancellor Nigel Lawson's argument that macro-economic policy should be aimed at countering inflation, not producing growth. In its micro-economic policy, the government could produce conditions conducive to growth, but it could not engage in Keynesian policies designed to stimulate demand and thus growth.

To reduce the 'natural rate of unemployment', it was necessary to reduce the costs of hiring labour. Lawson sought to do this by weakening the trade unions and reducing wages. Brown's emphasis was on equalising the endowment of skills and education that entrants to the labour market possessed, thus improving productivity. However, keeping the cost of hiring labour low also meant keeping flexible labour markets with minimal protections for British workers. It meant opting out of some basic protections for workers embedded in EU legislation. It meant keeping the anti-union laws, recently used to thwart strikes by BA cabin crew and railway workers, in place. Tony Blair boasted in 1997 that British employment law would remain "the most restrictive on trade unions in the western world." The net result of this approach under both Tory and Labour administrations was that wages stagnated, while the share of output going to profits increased. In redirecting its goals toward meritocracy, Labour sided with the employers in its struggle with workers over the distribution of the social product, and thus inequality was bound to rise.[97]

End of the affair

The government's love affair with the rich, we are assured, is over. This is because when the financial crisis struck, and the government found itself incurring public debt to pay for a bailout for the banks, New Labour applied slightly higher taxes on the wealthy and pushed for a modest global tax on the banks.[98] Raising taxes for high earners was a popular move, if a rather modest and diffident one, in the direction of redistribution. It was precious little compared to the public spending cuts that, deferred until after the 2010 election, all parties will impose, but it was well received by the public. However, having for years flattered the 'wealth creators', New Labour now found themselves on the end of a stream of ceaseless invective on behalf of the oppressed investor, the downtrodden banker, and the persecuted entrepreneur.

Andrew Lloyd Webber, in response to the new 50% income tax rate for those earning more than £100,000, complained that it would precipitate an "exodus of talent". "The last thing we need," he explained with the melodramatic sentimentality that has made him famous, "is a Somali pirate-style raid on the few wealth creators who still dare to navigate Britain's gale force waters".[9]

The rich under New Labour had become so self-righteous about their wealth accumulation that they considered even the smallest abridgement of it a betrayal and an act of criminal expropriation akin to high seas piracy. New Labour has now incurred the wrath of dozens of businessmen over a plan to raise national insurance contributions by an insignificant amount. They have flounced into the arms of the Conservative Party, in a strop over the perceived sleight. This despite all that New Labour has done for them, and despite the fact that last year the richest 1,000 Britons saw a record increase in their wealth due to the government pouring hundreds of billions of pounds into the banking system to prop up stock market and property values.[100]

At the same time, the rich have grown so contemptuous of the under-achieving poor that they are beginning to yearn for a return of the Victorian Poor Laws. The ex-head of the CBI and former New Labour minister Lord Digby Jones has argued that the government should "starve the jobless back to work", thus not only signalling a new level of ruling class viciousness, but also implying that mass unemployment in the middle of a recession is voluntary. He has argued that anyone who is unemployed should be forced to carry out community work, and anyone who refuses three job offers should be forced to live in a hostel on "subsistence rations".[101] One could hardly invent a more grotesque parody of capitalist self-righteousness, avarice, vindictive malice and stupidity. A polite word for it would be 'Dickensian'.

New Labour now campaigns in a losing election on the message that its opponents are in the pockets of the rich. This is, well, rich. New Labour celebrated its relationship with the plutocracy with all the boundless energy of a five year old on a sugar high. It cannot now profess to be prolier-than-thou. And it shows no sign of having actually learned anything. Its 2010 manifesto shows that it remains committed to the ideology of 'meritocracy'. It has one paragraph about the trade unions, which makes no commitments on their behalf. New Labour still admires the entrepreneurs, remains committed to maintaining profitable investment conditions for them at the expense of the working classes. And it is readying itself to introduce the deepest public spending cuts for decades. Deserted by rich and poor at the same time, squeezed to third place in the polls – if ever a party deserved to lose all of its friends at once, it is New Labour.

Conclusion

I have argued that meritocracy is a language of class rule, in three ways. Firstly, it validates the *principle of inequality* by reinterpreting privilege as merit. Secondly, it legitimises the *actually existing class system*, insofar as most capitalist societies represent themselves as being meritocratic with no fixed class boundaries holding people back. And thirdly, it encourages people to seek individual rather than class-based solutions to social problems. It is also an undesirable ideal in itself.

I have noted that New Labour was not prepared to take the radical measures necessary to create a mature meritocracy. But it is perhaps as well that they did not try to. The way 'merit' is used in everyday language, it is clear that it refers to individuals productively exercising their native abilities. Yet, only the most extreme Social Darwinists actually take this to its logical conclusion. After all, the implication is that in some sense one 'deserves' one's talents and thus any material rewards that might emanate from them. By logical corollary, those who lack special talents, or who are disabled in body or mind, deserve their disadvantage. From whence does such 'desert' arise? Karma? Perhaps, when the former manager of the England football team, Glen Hoddle, spoke of the disabled paying for sins in a previous life, he was speaking for more people than he knew.

To conflate political justice with biology in this way is obviously incompatible with any egalitarian agenda. It is inherently bound up with conservative discourses of hierarchy and domination, and the Left will stand a better chance of resisting any Tory recidivism if it junks the dogma of 'meritocracy' and the New Labour horse it rode in on.

Chapter Three

'Progress'

There is a tendency to put 'progressive' Tory rhetoric down to legerdemain, and there is undoubtedly some truth in this. As often as Cameron has extolled progress, he has championed traditionalist conservatism. He is, for example, explicit in his Burkean scepticism toward rationalist social doctrines, and his view, shared with Disraeli, that social transformation must be gradual and in accord with the "customs and manners and traditions and sentiments of the people rather than change according to some grand plan".[102] Given his attachment to such conventional Tory thought, which he describes as "brilliant", and his insistence on coterminously banging the gong of "progress", some uncharitable observers might draw the conclusion that he understands neither conservatism nor progressivism. Further, there is an element of platitude to describing oneself as a progressive in this era. It is a rare political animal who will stand before the public and boldly extol the wilful obstruction of progress, or declare herself to be proudly backward looking. Nevertheless, that leaves us with the task of understanding how such an apparently contradictory idea as progressive conservatism is intelligible in the first place. And there is a story here, which places forward-looking Cameronism in an interesting light.

The 'Party of Modernity'
Conservatism, so we are told, is a political philosophy grounded in a preference for the known and the familiar. It is traditional, it approaches change reluctantly and gradually, and it values the accumulated wisdom of existing institutions. Such is the account

of conservatism given by Tories from Burke to Disraeli to Oakeshott. So much for this – conservatives have always, in practise, been the enemies of tradition, adventurist, opportunistic and, where it suits their purposes, rabble-rousing. To say that conservatism amounts to a predisposition toward tradition is not only to misunderstand it, but it is to defame it in a way. As Ted Honderich points out, it would imply that conservatives fail to make the basic distinction between what is familiar and good, and what is familiar and bad. It would imply that conservatives have no consistent principles, and that they defend institutions they despised only some short time ago only because they have become familiar.[103]

The confusion of conservatism with traditionalism is shared by some on the Left. The radical sociologist C Wright Mills, drawing on Karl Mannheim's essay "Conservative Thought", argued that conservatism is "traditionalism become self-conscious and elaborated and forensic". But in fact, Mannheim's case was a little different. He certainly argued that *romanticism* emerged as a reaction to the rationalist bourgeois life-world of capitalism, recovering the submerged spiritual and cultural remnants of the feudal order. However, romanticism need not necessarily be right-wing. And Mannheim pointedly argued that there is no logical or necessary relationship between political conservatism and traditionalism. Rather, conservative action was "always dependent on *a concrete set of circumstances*" (emphasis in original).[104]

The political theorist Corey Robin thus argues that conservatism, as an ideology of reaction – first against the French revolution, subsequently against abolitionism, the extension of the franchise, communism, social democracy, Sixties liberalism, etc. – is fundamentally not about tradition, but about authority and hierarchy. It emerges in response to the Left's demands for freedom and equality, and whether it defends tradition or seeks to overthrow tradition, what it conserves is domination and inequality. In its formal ideological expressions, it has always been a pastiche of the traditional and the modern. Conservatives could not simply continue the tradition of the ancient regime, if they were to preserve it: indeed, their greatest invective was often directed toward the decrepitude of the old rulers. They had to adopt the insights, the habits of thought and the means of organising pioneered by their revolutionary opponents. Rather than simply foreswearing modernity, they had to articulate their own particular version of modernity. Rather than relying on tradition, they had to invent old hierarchies anew:

> Where their predecessors in the old regime thought of inequality as a naturally occurring phenomenon, an inheritance passed on from generation to generation, the conservatives' encounter with revolution teaches them that the revolutionaries were right after all: inequality is a human creation. And if it can be un-created by men and women, it can be recreated by men and women.
>
> "Citizens!" exclaims Maistre at the end of Considerations on France. "This is how counter-revolutions are made." Under the old regime, monarchy – like patriarchy, like Jim Crow – isn't made. It just is. It would be difficult to imagine a Loyseau or Bossuet declaring, "Men" – much less citizens – "this is how a monarchy is made." But once the old regime is threatened or toppled, the conservative is forced to the realisation that it is human agency, the willed imposition of intellect and imagination upon the world, that generates and maintains inequality across time.[105]

That the Tories should so avidly seek the 'progressive' mantle is not, therefore, as novel as it may appear in light of a certain clichéd view of conservatism. The twentieth century reaction against all forms of collectivism, whether socialist or social democratic, often represented itself as a defence of modernity.

The author Dan Hind has ironically referred to the right-wing liberals around Friedrich Hayek, and their free market successors, as the 'Party of Modernity'. Indeed, for Hayek and his epigones, the sole alternative to liberal capitalism is a pre-modern social form – all roads bar one lead to serfdom. It is striking just how much established powers, chiefly corporations and governments, seek to legitimise themselves with the language of modernity, with their opponents represented as medieval reactionaries or, when a more imaginative metaphor fails to occur, 'dinosaurs'.[106]

The Tories are taking advantage of an ideological realignment that was achieved partly by Thatcher and partly by the collapse of the USSR. If 'progress' had previously had something to do with socialism, or at least with the advance of the working class, the transition to a period in which both socialism and class were increasingly regarded as passé by the mainstream Left meant that 'progress' acquired new connotations. This political transubstantiation was facilitated in part by the ideology of 'postmodernity', in which such 'grand narratives' as class and the emancipatory politics that went with it were regarded as artificial totalisations of a plural and fragmentary social reality. Perry Anderson has argued, in his anatomy of *The Origins of Postmodernity*, that it is "a normal fate of strategic concepts to be subject to unexpected political capture and reversal".[107] The Tory raid on the language of progress is an attempt at just this kind of appropriation.

"Beyond Left and Right" (*translation*: Beyond Left)
The weltanschauung winds blow west
During New Labour's halcyon days, 'Third Way' social theorists celebrated the transition to a world that was 'beyond left and right'. Anthony Giddens, *en route* to establishing himself as Tony Blair's court philosopher, outlined the principles underlying this claim. Socialism, as classically understood, was moribund.

The red pole star of the Spasskaya Tower, overlooking Red Square, had once guided socialists as they navigated their way out of capitalism – but in the end, escape had proved both impossible and undesirable. (Giddens wasted little time despatching the anti-Stalinist left – their case, that the Stalinist dictatorship represented the defeat of the Russian revolution rather than the consummation of it, was curtly dismissed as "threadbare indeed").

Globalisation had undermined the Keynesian welfare state by allowing capital to side-step the restrictions of national states and move production overseas, thus finishing off socialism in its reformist variant. Unable to establish socialism either by parliamentary or revolutionary means, therefore, the left was increasingly in a conservative position of defending existing welfare settlements at the expense of any emancipatory project. By contrast, conservatives' embrace of global capitalism placed them with the radicals, tearing down tradition in the name of unfettered competition. If radical politics was to survive, its principal agents – the remaining social democratic parties – would have to abandon the traditional orientations of the left, and embrace modernising processes of globalisation while seeking to mitigate their effects and prevent the emergence of fundamentalisms.[108] This analysis is susceptible to the critique outlined above. The right was never especially partial to tradition, where tradition failed to protect a social order predicated on domination and hierarchy. The left, in defending traditional welfare and public services, is not thereby becoming conservative.

Still, Giddens was expressing one version of a conclusion that had been widely reached, and it is only fair to point out that the despondency of many on the Left in the face of the 'new world order' was shared by some on the right. Neoconservatives were particularly unhappy. All those Free Worlders with nowhere left to free – on whose lawns would they park their think-tanks now?

The world really did seem to be moving beyond ideology, beyond class, and beyond nation-states. Arthur Jensen's evangel was being realised right before their eyes, and it depressed them terribly. Francis Fukuyama, who would go on to align himself with the neoconservative right and sign up to the Project for the New American Century, scrutinised the tea-leaves and deciphered 'the End of History'. With the conclusive victory of liberal capitalism, all that remained of the thriving life forms of *kultur* gave way to the bourgeois rigidities of *zivilisation*.[109] He and the remainder of the neoconservatives spent the 1990s yearning for the kind of adventure that only an empire could bring. And through their advocacy over the former Yugoslavia, they started to develop relationships with liberals and former leftists who would, in future years, share their passion for conquest and give it a progressive seal.

Atlanticism and Blair's progressive century

Tony Blair's conception of 'progress' was profoundly informed by Third Way intellectuals. These included not just Anthony Giddens, but also Geoff Mulgan, the founder of the Third Way think-tank Demos, Gordon Brown's adviser in the 1990s and subsequently Blair's policy director. He was also impressed by the 'Third Way' politics embraced by the Australian Labour Party in the 1980s, and by the 'New Democrats' in the United States, a neoliberal faction of the Democratic Party based in the Democratic Leadership Council.[110]

This was a logical affinity for the Blairites, whose Atlanticism was continuous with that of the old Labour Right, and the SDP. There was a legacy of CIA intervention into Labour Party politics, designed to bolster its anti-socialist right-wing, not just through the Congress for Cultural Freedom which had attracted figures from the old Labour Right such as Hugh Gaitskell and Roy Jenkins, but also through surveillance and penetration of British trade unions, and acquiring assets in the UK's own

Information Research Department, a body set up by the Foreign Office to agitate against communism and its fellow-travellers. The US Labour Attaché was also able to exert influence on policymaking in Labour administrations, and helped direct campaigns against the Left.

What Robin Ramsay has called "the American Tendency" within Labour was also central to the project of developing first the Social Democratic Alliance, a right-wing pressure group within Labour, and then the SDP. This tendency was also represented in the British American Project, created in 1985 to help institutionalise and perpetuate the 'special relationship', and which has included among its supporters such New Labour votaries as Peter Mandelson, Geoff Mulgan, Jonathan Powell (who later helped rig the infamous Iraq weapons dossier) and George Robertson. It was in the course of repeated visits to the US in the 1980s and early 1990s that Tony Blair and Gordon Brown forged their relationships not only with the 'New Democrats' but also with American businesses who agreed to fund their visits.[111]

It is worth noting the similarity of experiences that made for such a symbiosis between New Labour and New Democrat. Just as the Blairites gained from the Labour Party's repeated electoral maulings, so the New Democrats had emerged in response to Reagan's successes in the 1980s. They argued that the old progressive coalition of middle class liberals, blue collar workers and particularly African Americans was breaking up, and that there wasn't a majority for New Deal policies any more. There were dynamics internal to Democratic Party politics that favoured their ascendancy. The left of the Democratic Party, which had backed Jesse Jackson's 'rainbow coalition' in the 1984 primaries, while gaining 80% of African American voters, was able to muster only 19% of all primary votes. Given that the Reaganites had won in 1980 by playing to segregationists and southern reactionaries, which was the major social force behind the Christian Right, it was reasonably inferred that a substantial number of white voters had moved to the right in reaction to the civil rights reforms of the Sixties. The old New Deal centre - which was represented by Walter Mondale, and supported by the AFL-CIO, many white liberals and a sector of capital - had won the Democratic machinery but had lost to Reagan in a landslide, in which the incumbent won almost 60% of the votes. Michael Dukakis' moderate liberal campaign in 1988 was also defeated by a wide margin, especially after the 'Willie Horton' campaign ad, which summoned white dread of black rapists and murderers being freed from prison by the bleeding-hearts only to kill again.[112]

Thus, the New Democrats, representing the most right-wing elements in the Democratic Party, uniting southern conservatives with neoliberals, supported Bill Clinton's presidential bid, and were influential in his policymaking. Welfare reform, for example, was a key priority for Third Way Democrats. Undoing the New Deal that had underpinned the Democrats' reputation for progressive social reform, they said that welfare must be replaced by 'workfare', wherein a recipient of state benefits was required to work. It was a reinvention of the Victorian Poor Laws, supplying poverty employers with an intimidated labour force whose productivity would be sharply increased by the threat of having their income cut off. By 2006, Clinton was vaunting his success in his this regard, regaling well-to-do *New York Times* readers with the tale of 'How We Ended Welfare, Together'.[113]

It was also the New Democrats who pioneered the rightly reviled idea of privatising social security, breaking up the efficient public sector programme and turning some of it into a series of individual accounts managed by Wall Street. It was they who opposed minimum wage increases and, in the person of Senator Joseph Lieberman (now an Independent), begged Clinton to go further in marketising the system of welfare entitlements.[114] Even Clinton's moderately reformist agenda fell victim to the logic of the neoliberal state. Shortly after his election, he was told by a claque of neoliberal economists that his reforms package – involving, among other things, the funding of education and training to improve labour productivity – would have to be cancelled. He had to cut the budget by $140 billion otherwise he would lose the confidence of Wall Street, the economy would tank, and his administration would go under with it. "You mean to tell me," he exploded, "that the success of my program and my re-election hinges on the Federal Reserve and a bunch of fucking bond dealers?" Answer: yes. After his inauguration, he again raged at having to jettison his limited commitments, declaring that the Democrats had become "Eisenhower Republicans" who stood for low deficits and bond markets.[115]

The legitimacy of any executive, from there on, was to be based exclusively on economic growth – *It's the economy, stupid!*, as the Democrats campaign slogan had it – and that growth was obtained through reduced spending, privatisation, low deficits and a happy stock market. Clinton acquiesced, and economic policy was entrusted to a former Goldman Sachs banker and Alan Greenspan, setting a precedent that Bush *fils* would emulate.

New antinomies of progress
By the time New Labour was invented, launched and on the electoral market, the lessons that Clinton had to absorb after being elected had already been assimilated by Tony Blair and his advisors. Nothing could be done without winning over business and the corporate media. No reform could be attempted that didn't have the blessing of someone from the CBI, or the Institute of Directors, or the City of London. The co-ordinates for New Labour's economic policy were clearly articulated by Brown: there would be an independent Bank of England, fiscal

'prudence', no borrowing to support current spending, a light regulatory touch, and no sudden increases in taxes on income, property or profits. In this way, a stable investment climate would be obtained. Welfare reform would also be introduced, modelled on the principle of 'welfare to work' pioneered not by New Labour or even the Clintons, but by Margaret Thatcher. Welfare-to-work was a Tory policy and the Tories – not New Labour – launched the first such scheme with 'Project Work' in 1996.[116]

The progressive agenda was thus one which the Conservative Party could have few substantive objections to. After all, Blair was explicit: the 21st Century was to be a struggle not between socialism and capitalism – "the class war is over", he insisted – but between "progress" and the "forces of conservatism". The latter included not just the xenophobic Tory Right, but particularly the Left, and the unions whom he would later castigate as "wreckers" when they opposed his privatisation agenda. Pace Giddens, the defining issue of the new century was 'globalisation'. The term implied a process that was taking place independently of human agency. But it referred to a series of dramatic changes in regulatory regimes, property laws, taxes, exchange controls and employment codes – almost all to the benefit of capital and to the detriment of labour – as well as the institutionalisation of neoliberal policies at an international level, principally through the World Trade Organisation. New Labour, declaring the inability of the nation-state to resist such changes, insisted that the correct approach was to adapt to them and make them work for social justice.[117] It followed that the endorsement of market-driven solutions to public service delivery and 'social exclusion' was both progressive and pragmatic – though such pragmatism was always susceptible to J M Keynes' rebuke: "Practical men, who believe themselves to be quite exempt from any intellectual influence, are usually the slaves of some defunct economist."[118]

Implicit in Blair's argument was a sort of blackmail. Politicians often tell us that we mustn't pass legislation that will offend the rich, as they will take their capital and invest it elsewhere. This threat of capital flight, in which businesses could transport investment and jobs to Mexico, or India, or Indonesia, has been a key means of disciplining labour markets and electorates. It forced them to accept a particular form of 'realism', that being that you can't buck the market, and that there is no alternative. Blair, by saying that it was not possible to stop or reverse the processes of 'globalisation', implied that the state's democratic capacities had been seriously curtailed by the international mobility of capital. Thus, there was no alternative to pursuing pro-business policies, and adapting to the changes they demanded. In fact, the international mobility of capital was always hugely over-stated[119], and most jobs that have been lost in the era of 'globalisation' have been shed by downsizing rather than outsourcing. However, the way in which this idea is used to bolster the power of capital in wage bargaining and in the political process belies the argument that 'the class war is over'.

Progress asserted itself most forcefully, however, in its imperial guise. New Labour's Atlanticist orientations would lead the party into supporting American wars in Yugoslavia and Afghanistan on ostensibly humanitarian grounds. In justifying these wars, Tony Blair offered the 'doctrine of the international community'. In this doctrine, it was the responsibility of Western states to be guided by, as it were, 'enlightened self-interest'. That is, the 'mutual self-interest' of Western states was best defended when they aggrandised their Enlightened 'values'. The spread of a liberal world order, made possible by the collapse of the USSR, was both morally just and a material interest worth pursuing.[120] For a number of former left-wingers, this was an attractive doctrine. If they had once believed that the Soviet Union or the working class was the vanguard of global progress, it was now possible for them to see liberal capitalism as its bulwark. If the battle was between cosmopolitan, liberal modernity on the one hand, and various fundamentalist or nationalist challenges on the other, then progressives would take the side of modernity.

That this was reheated Gladstonian 'moral' imperialism – 'traditional values in a modern setting,' if you like – was neither here nor there, so long as the designated opponents were indeed lacking in liberal values, and provided the wars were brief and ⸱⸱⸱lties relatively few. However, signing up to a global ⸱⸱⸱us of secret prisons, torture, extraordinary rendition ⸱⸱⸱ ⸱ost egregiously, the adventurist invasion and occupation ⸱⸱ ⸱⸱ ıq, was a different matter. I have written elsewhere about the liberal cheerleaders who provided a certain progressive respectability for Operation Iraqi Freedom.[121] But New Labour's role was crucial in this respect. Absent Blair's support, and that of his parliamentary party, and it is difficult to see how such a venture could have been sold as anything but a reactionary venture. This divided the liberal and social democratic coalition that had supported New Labour's previous displays of British martial arts, and it tested New Labour's electoral coalition by sending antiwar Labour supporters into the arms of the Liberal Democrats, the nationalist parties and in some instances the radical Left. It also divided the continental centre-left, meaning that New Labour's alliance with the American right also forced it to rely increasingly on leaders of the European right, such as Silvio Berlusconi and Nicolas Sarkozy. It pushed Labour even closer to the Tories than they had previously been. And as we will see, all of those threads of progress running from Thatcher to Blair are now woven into the Cameronite tapestry.

The Tories Get Medieval
'Big Society': in which all the world is a market and all the men and women merely consumers
The watch-words of the Tories' electoral campaign are

mutualism, cooperative enterprise, and voluntary association. They allege that the state has failed, and 'Big Government' must give way to 'Big Society'. Services and welfare are best delivered by non-governmental institutions and social entrepreneurs. The users of public services must be able to choose from different providers. Centrally dictated targets must be abolished, and layers of bureaucracy and management blitzed. In fact, this is a straightforward encroachment on what has been New Labour territory for more than a decade. It was Gordon Brown who, in 2000, said that while the state had once had to accumulate power to tackle social injustice, "to tackle the social injustices that still remain the state will have to give power away".[122] Delegating state functions through market-based mechanisms has been a New Labour hallmark. 'Devolution to the front-line', the de-centralisation of decision-making, 'choice', and 'consumer sensitivity' have been bromides of Blairite rule.[123]

Another way to put this would be to say that the Conservatives are invading their *own* turf. Previous Tory manifestos, offered as explicitly rightist programmes, contained very similar policies. For example, the policy enabling residents to force a referendum on council tax rises revisits the 2001 manifesto. The tax break for married couples was in the 1997, 2001 and 2005 manifestos, the latter of which was co-drafted by David Cameron. 'Efficiency savings', to be achieved by removing layers of 'bureaucracy', cutting hundreds of thousands of civil service posts and incentivising 'excellence', were promised in previous manifestos. And once again, such rationalisation and down-sizing of the state was already being carried out by New Labour, and had already led to several confrontations with the PCS union.[124]

All of these policies, I need hardly say, are impeccably neoliberal. Yet what is distinctive about the Cameronites is that they appear to offer the same policies in language that claims to be sceptical toward neoliberalism. This is where the phenomenon of 'Red Toryism' comes in. Modelled on the Canadian trend, Red Toryism, whose most notable UK exponent is Phillip Blond, professes to be socially conservative while being willing to use the state to curtail private sector 'greed'. Fulfilling much the same function as Third Way intellectuals did for Tony Blair, Blond has emerged as David Cameron's sidekick sage, a conservative cogitator who provides a similitude of intellectual coherence to the often *ad hoc* policy formulae of his masters while maintaining a minimum of critical distance. He is one of the loudest exponents of the underlying principles behind the 'big society', which impeaches both "the unrestrained market and the unlimited state" on behalf of family, community and civic association. It offers a conservatism which, he claims, has "deeper roots than 1979."[125] Is this roots treatment merely cosmetic, or is it surgical?

To answer this, it is necessary to look briefly at how deep the roots of Red Toryism go. This is not a simple matter, for a number of critics have noted an occult quality to Blond's writing. He does not own up to his intellectual antecedents, is nebulous about his influences, and downright obscure about the philosophical premises of his social purview. It is clear that he is hostile, not just to neoliberalism, but liberalism of all kinds. It is clear that he does not believe that human beings are simply the rational-economic actors that liberal theory takes them for. He is opposed to individualism, and permissiveness. He is explicit about wishing to disrupt and reverse the integration of the global economy, mutualise companies, downscale enterprise to family or community-sized units, and break up the supermarket chains. As for the state, its role – having broken up the large corporations, redistributed wealth in order to 'recapitalise' the working class, disaggregated global trading networks and launched a moral revolution - is to dismantle itself. But what precepts underpin his recommendations is less clear.

Thus, Nathan Coombs has written of an "esoteric political

theology" underwriting the Red Tory project, which he relates to a Catholic theological current known as 'Radical Orthodoxy'. This current, though informed by postmodern philosophy, is hostile to liberalism and secularism, and favours a 'return' to medieval and patristic roots.[126] Theological and anti-secularist concerns, it should be added, were more explicit in Blond's pre-Cameron days. Writing with Adrian Pabst in the *New York Times* in 2005, only weeks after the 7/7 attacks, he aligned himself with the rhapsodists of civilisational clash, by execrating Islam as the authentic source of terrorism (while also finding a way to incriminate secularism and liberalism). Pabst and Blond did not believe a 'war on terror' could work, but they did insist that Islam needed a reformation, though in fact their own common-place analogy of Wahabbism with Protestantism suggests that it has already had one.

Later, he and Pabst argued that liberal multiculturalism had failed to 'integrate' Muslims, and that only a full restoration of the dominant social role of Europe's "indigenous" (sic) religious tradition would achieve this. Quite why they would wish to integrate a religious community whose beliefs they hold respon-sible for Al Qaeda is mysterious. And it would be rude to suggest that their own indictment of Islam might not have been a constructive contribution to harmonious 'integration'. But it could at least be said that for all that multiculturalism failed to end discrimination, Muslims were not safer in Europe when sacred power was dominant. Quite the reverse.[127]

But theology is not the end of the story. Jonathan Raban, in a cheerfully contemptuous dispatch, alerted would-be readers of Blond's book, *Red Tory*, to the understated influence of G K Chesterton and Hilaire Belloc.[128] Thus, the localism and preference for small-scale enterprise owes itself to the doctrine of distributism originated by Chesterton and Belloc in the early twentieth century. It is an influence that Blond has reason to be coy about, since the founders of distributism also had radical right sympathies (fascist sympathies in Belloc's case) that would have placed them at odds with 'progressive' Toryism. But it is evident that his entire political philosophy leans heavily on Chesterton's 1921 'Distributist Manifesto', which championed the smallholder and the yeoman farmer against the Marxists, the state and the monopolists.

More embarrassing still, perhaps, is that the pseudo-bucolic society that it aims for is hopelessly unrealistic, the means voluntarist and not predicated on any analysis of the potencies within the society it seeks to overthrow. It seeks an artisanal Arcadia which would universalise the petit-bourgeois mode of living, but shows no sign of having located an agency by which this could happen. Coombs rightly argues that Blond is expecting members of a financial and industrial elite to enter the state, act against their own class interests by liquidating the very forms of mass capitalist production and global financial exchanges that they are embedded in, and then liquidate the state through which they accomplished this act of self-expropriation. Such obscurantist thinking is embedded in the original distributist project. For, in contrast to how conservatism usually represents itself, distributism was explicitly utopian in its foundation. It was revolutionary, Corey Robin argues, in the sense that it believed that it was possible to radically overhaul society and re-order temporality. Its desired end-state was a sort of 'Year Zero'; not so much 'Red Toryism', then, as Khmer Rouge conservatism.[129]

Of course, Cameron has no intention of making good on Blond's progressive medievalism. Blond, in seeking the patronage of the Cameronites, has offered them one means by which to affect that strategic capture of the language of progress that I mentioned earlier. The idea that Cameron would break up the large enterprises that are supporting his election, expropriate the people who are funding his campaign (not to mention his friends and members of his shadow cabinet), or otherwise fundamentally attack the class structure in Britain is fantastical. The issue underlying these ideological torsions, which is not discussed in polite company, is the neoliberal state – or, the "competition state", as Mark Evans has dubbed it.[130]

Evans claims, correctly in my view, that Brown's current use of Keynesian demand management and stimulus is no more than a transitory form of crisis management, and does not signal a paradigm shift. A neoliberalism with a tighter regulatory regime and a much diminished welfare state and public sector is far more likely in the future. The processes that have been 'hollowing-out' the state, depriving it of democratic capacity by devolving ministerial powers to unelected agencies or privatised entities, or to unelected EU bodies, will continue largely as a result of this underlying neoliberal commitment.

That the Tories' proposals to further erode representative democracy should themselves be expounded in the vernacular of democratic renewal reflects sensitivity on this issue. The Tories are aware, as Westminster's mandarins are also aware[131], that the undermining of the state's representative capacity is producing a severe decline in the public's faith in, and thus the legitimacy of, the state. Their only logical way of handling this is to try to persuade the public that this undermining of democracy is precisely the kind of democratisation that they really want. And for the Tories to do this credibly, they can't do it as open Thatcherites. Hence, the need to find a 'progressive' idiom; hence the hopey-changey, touchy-feely, happy-clappy Sunday school rhetoric; and hence the painfully inept attempt by Cameron – and now also by Nick Clegg – at a kind of 'Stars in Their Eyes' Obama impersonation.

Neoconservatives: the American Lobby

Speaking of Obama, it is rather fortunate that he arrived on time. The Tories have been anxious to forge their own particular relationship with the United States government and its current global strategy (no longer officially promulgated under the rubric of the 'war on terror'). And while their affiliations were with the Republican administration, Obama is both more attractive and poses no ideological problems for cooperation with a Cameron government. This is important because the Tories aim for continuity with the previous government in foreign policy. A recent study of Conservative foreign policy noted that "since 11 September 2001 the Conservative party has not presented a radically different interpretation of world events from Labour". The party, it explained, was having diffi-culty developing distinctive ideas on Britain's overseas posture, and had failed to regain its old lead over Labour on that issue despite the unpopularity of the invasion of Iraq. Cameron's foreign policy announcements have been either "trite" or unoriginal.[132]

The basic posture of Conservative foreign policy has been worked out between David Cameron and William Hague. The Tories, they say, will pursue a "liberal conservative" policy, with idealism "tempered by realism". "Liberal interventionism", they hold, is a good policy, even if New Labour has not always implemented it ideally. Though it is difficult for the Tories to disagree with Labour on any of its actual policies, and though their rhetoric is strikingly similar to Blair's, they argue that the manner in which policy is made is one key area in which they can differentiate themselves from Blair.[133] In this respect, their sole unique selling point on foreign policy is the promise to create a national security council, run by the shadow security minister Dame Pauline Neville-Jones, to coordinate war planning. This is weak tea, and a particularly poor effort given that foreign policy is one of the issues on which Labour is most vulnerable.

But in fact, this was inevitable. The Tories whom Cameron has surrounded himself with are largely those who viewed Blair's Churchillian bluster with admiring envy. The neoconservative Michael Gove, promoted to the shadow cabinet by David Cameron and one of his closest allies, was explicit on this point. During the build up to the Iraq war, he enthused about the "outstanding" Tony Blair, declaring: "I can't fight my feelings any more: I love Tony". It was not just the stance on Iraq that attracted his admiration: it was also his handling of asylum, the firefighters' strike, his disdain for European human rights legislation, and his imposition of unpopular tuition fees that commanded adoration. But above all, on foreign policy, Blair was "behaving like a true Thatcherite".[134]

Ed Vaisey, another neoconservative in Cameron's court is also, like Gove, a signatory to the Henry Jackson Society, a neoconservative lobby which is supported by both Labour and Conservative politicians as well as by Cameron's former lecturer, Vernon Bogdanor.[135] Similarly, the shadow chancellor George Osborne remains a "signed up, card-carrying Bush fan," persuaded of the "excellent neoconservative case" for war with Iraq. The former Tory leader Michael Howard went even farther. He would have invaded Iraq even if he knew there were no WMD, a position that Blair has also recently articulated.[136] Here, the overlap between the (exoteric) vocabulary of neoconservatives and that of liberal interventionists is obvious. And it could be argued that this comradeship-in-arms restores a unity that was lost when the Cold War consensus fragmented over Vietnam.

On Iraq, Cameron himself, though traditionally pro-American, tried to signal a slightly nuanced approach. He declared himself, as his postbag bulged with antiwar letters from outraged suburban constituents, "confused and uncertain". He had expressed profound scepticism about the idea that Saddam Hussein had weapons of mass destruction or Al Qaeda links, and saw no reason not to rely on deterrence as opposed to invasion. In the end, however, he voted for the war, "grudgingly, unhappily, unenthusiastically". This was not because he had been convinced of the case for war, but principally because to vote against war would be to attack the US-UK relationship which was "at the heart of NATO". He weakly suggested that to abandon the US now would ensure that it would never again pursue multilateralism in foreign affairs, thus implying that caving in to the Bush administration gave the UK government leverage over US policy in future. And, like his present cabinet allies, he could not hide his agape awe of Prime Minister Blair, who had been "masterful".[137]

The Tories' commitment to the 'special relationship', which the British state has been locked into since 1945, means they are committing themselves to an unpopular and costly occupation of Afghanistan at precisely a time when they anticipate making spending cuts. It means that they have bloodied themselves by association with the Iraq war, and that disaffection with Labour over its foreign policy was never likely to redound to their advantage. 'Little England' sentiment is no help with this, since the Little Englanders have turned anti-war. No amount of saving the pound and Union Jack waving will arouse support for the increasing troop levels and investment that the conquest of Afghanistan and now Pakistan will require. At most, the Tories can land a few blows on the government for failing to properly equip Our Brave Boys. (I beg to demur from this popular designation, by the way: it is their opponents, mostly tribal people trying to resist an aggressive occupation with far more rudimentary equipment than the average British soldier has, who are brave).

As a result, the Tories' embrace of 'liberal interventionism', along with the moderation of their Europhobic agenda and the general disinclination to fall back on belligerent xenophobia, is a logical step, even if it means that their criticisms of the government can ultimately only be technocratic. Cameron can now boast a 'progressive', 'forward-looking', 21st Century foreign policy, however much it resembles a 19th Century throwback. He can claim a bipartisan consensus on the war in Afghanistan, and he can rely on New Labour ministers and intelligentsia to support him.

Conclusion

I have argued that the Conservative Party's 'progressive' discourse is far from aberrant in the history of conservative thought. I have maintained that the Tories' current ability to position themselves as progressive while upholding hard right policies on the economy, the state, and foreign policy, results from domestic and global transformations that appeared to alter the coordinates within which the meaning of terms such as progress was determined. I have also argued that a structural logic deeper than electoralism is driving the Tories to articulate their policies in this way. They need, of course, to soften their edges, distance themselves from Thatcherism, and appear to position themselves in the 'centre'.

But more than an electoral appeal, this language of market-driven progressivism is a language of statecraft. The logic of neoliberal accumulation, described in Chapter One, compels states to relentlessly continue to 'enclose' public assets, privatise and marketise them, and insulate them from genuine democratic accountability. At the same time, it ceaselessly attacks those 'traditions' that people have reason to value, however flawed they are. These include not only traditions of welfarism and trade unionism, but also basic civil liberties derived from the Magna Carta. It constantly seeks, usually with little success, to overturn people's basic value orientations, to acculturate them to new necessities such as prolonged wars, internment, kidnapping, and the revival practises of torture that were outlawed by European states in the 18th Century. In that light, neoliberalism is indeed dynamic and progressive. But that rather peculiar sense of progress should not be accepted at face value or confused with the project of political progress which, we ought to insist, is movement in the direction of political and economic equality, and away from class domination.

Conclusion

What, after all, is Cameronism? What is the *meaning* of David Cameron? In one sense, it is an electoral formula that speaks to the Tories' need to reach out well beyond their own class base - that being capital and a section of the middle class. They have donned a 'progressive', 'centrist' outfit, borrowing extensively from the New Labour wardrobe, out of electoral necessity. But that they can distance themselves from the Thatcher era while maintaining fidelity to its basic policy orientations is something that has been made possible by their Labour opponents. In another sense, Cameronism is a pragmatic adaptation to the needs of neoliberal statecraft. Neither Labour nor the Tories are at liberty to simply stop the 'hollowing-out' of the state, its marketisation, rationalisation and downsizing, simply by fiat. Nor can they come out against the British state's alliance with the US, unless they intend to abandon their business allies and their supporters in the financial sector whose class power, as David Harvey has pointed out, was substantially created by the Tories' 1980s reforms.[138] And the Conservatives are increasingly constrained in their ability to oppose EU legislation that, while abridging the sovereignty of the British state and undermining the xenophobic right, is consistent with the neoliberal project. This is why Cameron's "cast iron guarantee" of a referendum on the EU Treaty turned to spineless capitulation.

I will risk a bet on the outcome of the upcoming election. Nick Clegg's nuptials with the electorate notwithstanding, Cameron is likely to win a plurality of the vote. This means he will probably get a small working majority of the seats with the support of around a third of the voting public. His mandate, insecure within his own party [139], will be weak in the country. His government, indeed any elected government, will have to engage in a major confrontation with everyone who stands to lose from the deep public sector cuts that are on their way, particularly the public sector workers. This is why David Cameron has constantly pleaded for voters to deliver a strong Tory mandate, and avoid a hung parliament. He doesn't require the support of a majority of the public, any more than Thatcher did, just enough votes in the right constituencies to give him a voting majority in parliament that will mean he is not too constrained by public pressure on Labour and Liberal Democrat MPs, who might thereby obstruct his agenda. Even if he gets his wish, it is a future fraught with deep peril for him. Mervyn King, former head of the Bank of England, has asserted that whoever wins the next election will be out of power for a generation after. Not for nothing, the writer John Lanchester calls the 2010 general election, "a good election to lose."[140]

Let us take a brief survey of the terrain which the Tories hope to command. As of writing, the UK had just edged out of recession, perhaps temporarily, with modest growth restored since June 2009. But most voters, if thus far insulated from the worst effects of the recession by stimulus spending, have yet to feel any benefit from this. This is because, over three quarters from June 2009 until April 2010, national income grew by £27bn, of which profits accounted for £24bn, and wages a mere £2bn. The chief executives and directors who had successfully delivered these profits for shareholders were duly rewarded – the chiefs of the FTSE 100 companies gained an average 125% pay rise, compounding a broader trend in which the average CEO has seen his income rise from being 47 times that of an average employee in 2000 to 81 times the average in 2010.

In 2010, the income of the thousand richest people in Britain, according to the Sunday Times, soared by a record 30%. Real income for most has been close to stagnant for a decade, less than 1% in the period from 2001. The official unemployment rate, using ILO definitions, was 7.8%, or 2.45m. The actual rate of unemployment was much higher - the working age employment rate was only 72.2%. Even if GDP growth continues, it is assumed that unemployment will continue to rise, especially as stimulus spending is removed and public spending cuts are imposed.[141] For the Tories to withdraw stimulus spending in a short, sharp shock, and slash the public sector, will probably energise and galvanise the trade unions and forces to his Left, although they will have to build considerably on their presently contracted social base in order to prevail against the Conservatives and a ruling class determined to see these cuts pushed through.

Meanwhile, the underlying structural imbalances that made the UK uniquely exposed to recession have not been rectified, and Cameron is not well-placed to address these even if it was on his agenda. Regulatory reform of the financial sector is being proposed by all the parties, but the Tories are notable for the timidity of their proposed reforms. In fact, timidity is the wrong word for it – they are aggressively seeking to enhance the power of the City. They are unwilling to demand that banks separate high-risk investment from low-risk retail banking. Their policy of strengthening the role of the Bank of England adds to the clout of the financial sector. And their proposal to delegate a specific Treasury minister to the European Union to fight regulations that are injurious to the City's activities only consolidates this tendency.[142]

And the social power of the financiers poses problems for even a Tory administration. The UK is still very vulnerable to a speculative attack along the lines of that which has plunged Greece into repeated crises. If the Tories are unable for any reason to implement their emergency budget once elected, bonds markets will lose confidence in the UK's ability to pay its debts, will drive up the 'yield' on UK government borrowing, meaning the UK Treasury will have to pay back its debts at higher rates of interest. That will eat even further into the funds available for public spending, and will mean that most new wealth created by any period of growth – supposing the economy hasn't slipped back into recession – will be spent on paying the debt.

There is a possibility that the UK, alongside other advanced economies, will have to default on its debts. But if they do so, it poses serious problems for the financialised economic model that they have pursued for thirty years. For example, the running down of state pensions and the promotion of private or occupational pension schemes that depend on stock market growth, means that millions of people would find their retirement in jeopardy in the case of a default. This isn't a problem that is unique to the UK. Recall that the neoliberal experiment began in Chile. Chile's privatised pension scheme, built on the advice of the 'Chicago Boys' inspired by Friedrich Hayek and Milton Friedman, has inspired emulous praise from George W Bush. It failed to cover 40% of the population, and gave only weak coverage to a further 40%. It has left retirees with huge shortfalls in their incomes, and has been susceptible to sudden deep cuts in value during the financial crisis.

Yet it presaged a wave of privatisation and commodification of pension schemes that has turned old age into an age of insecurity. Political pressure has forced all three major parties to concede that the value of pensions should be linked with earnings, but even when the British State Pension was linked with earnings, it was valued at only 20% of average earnings, meaning that anyone wanting to avoid a sudden reduction in their incomes tending toward penury would still have to obtain an occupational pension scheme or a private scheme. New Labour has based its pensions policies on a decline of public contributions to private pensions, offset by more private provision (for those who could afford it). Re-establishing the link with earnings is unlikely to reverse this long-term trend. Moreover, by agreeing to raise the state pension age well above the life expectancy in parts of Britain, all parties have ensured that many of the poorest will never see a pension, and those who want to retire before they die will have to have a private scheme.[143] This is a time bomb being visited on the present generation of workers, because no major party has an alternative to the politics of down-sizing and privatising the state.

The manufacturing sector has briefly benefited from low interest rates imposed by the Bank of England during the crisis. However, it remains smaller than when the recession began, and its decline is long-term. Between 1970 and 1995, the number of people employed in manufacturing fell by a half. Between 1995 and 2009, it fell again from approximately 4.5m to under 3m. Since manufacturing is the main source of exports for the UK economy, Britain has maintained a consistent balance of payments deficit. Spending on research and development remains below that of other economies, and a disproportionate amount of this comes from overseas investment. The car industry has, after some improvement due to foreign direct investment in the 1990s, continued a long-term decline in the 2000s as Vauxhall, Peugeot, Ford and MG Rover all closed plants – this despite an expansion of traffic on the roads in part due to longer work commutes and the run-down of public transport.[144] The subordinate position of the UK manufacturing sector relative to the service economy and particularly the politically powerful financial sector is one reason why the UK was particularly exposed to the financial crash that precipitated the global downturn.

Electorally, this has some important ramifications. In those areas where manufacturing was formerly strong, with unionised workforces underpinning Labour's electoral majorities, the collapse of manufacturing industries has decimated Labour's base. With employment strongholds removed, economic growth has been weak, unemployment higher than average, and tax receipts depressed for local councils. In many of these areas, a boycott by Labour voters, or a shift in their votes, could benefit the Liberal Democrats. More ominous, however, is the prospect of far right success. The British National Party, though not principally drawing votes from among former Labour supporters, – in fact, their support is disproportionately drawn from former Tories, both working class and lower middle class – has been able to thrive in these circumstances by attributing the manufacturing decline to immigration and foreign competition. The distribution of their strongholds in the north-east, Midlands and in the former Ford production centre of Barking and Dagenham, attests to this. The capacity of local Labour Party machines to resist this encroachment in their heartlands has been weakened by the fact that it is Labour itself that has been hacking at its own roots in these constituencies. It has fallen to coalitions of activists extending well beyond the Labour Party to mobilise against the BNP.

In all, Cameronism comes with irenic intonations, soothing, anaesthetising language about change, just at the time when an epochal social crisis with deep political polarisation is about to be visited on this unhappy island-state. Just as Margaret Thatcher launched a bellicose administration with a pacific quote from St Francis of Assissi, so David Cameron comes to us as an agent of discord, distress and social misery, with an olive branch thrust toward his opponents. What is the meaning of David Cameron? He means war.

Endnotes

Prologue

1 David Cameron, "Labour are now the reactionaries, we the radicals", *The Guardian*, 8 April 2010

2 David Cameron, "This is a radical revolt against the statist approach of Big Government", *The Observer*, 18 April 2010; Simon Lee & Matt Leech, *The Conservatives Under David Cameron: Built to Last?*, Palgrave Macmillan, 2009, pp. 52-56; George Osborne, 'My pledge to public sector workers', *The Guardian*, 16 April 2010

3 On Cameron's Thatcherite ideology, see Simon Lee & Matt Leech, *The Conservatives Under David Cameron: Built to Last?*, Palgrave Macmillan, 2009, pp. 51-52; For Cameron's views on immigration, multiculturalism, the royal family, family values and taxes, see Dylan Jones, *Cameron on Cameron: Conversations With Dylan Jones*, Fourth Estate, London, 2008; For the New Labour-friendly reaction to Cameron's "progressive" agenda, see Polly Toynbee, "Beware the 'radical' Tories. The reality is terrifying", *The Guardian*, 10 April 2010

4 Mike Brewer, Alastair Muriel, David Phillips & Luke Sibieta, "Poverty and Income Inequality in the UK: 2009", *Institute for Fiscal Studies*, May 2009 <http://www.ifs.org.uk /comms/ c109.pdf>

5 Randeep Ramesh, "Britain in 2010: More tolerant, more Conservative, but less likely to vote", *The Guardian*, 26 January 2010

6 Tony Wood, "Good Riddance to New Labour", *New Left Review* 62, March-April 2010; Hélène Mulholland and Patrick Wintour, 'Gordon Brown admits banks needed more regulation', *The Guardian*, 14 April 2010

7 John Ramsden, *An Appetite for Power: A History of the Conservative Party Since 1830*, HarperCollins, 1998; Paul

Whiteley, Patrick Seyd & Jeremy John Richardson, *True Blues: the politics of Conservative Party membership*, Oxford University Press, 1994; Susan Watkins, "Toryism After Blair", *New Left Review* 38, March/April 2006

8   An informal clique of senior Tories who selected party leaders without the input of the constituency or parliamentary party, abolished in 1965 when the parliamentary party was allowed to elect its leader for the first time.

9   Polls suggest that of all social groups, more voters expect a Conservative government to assist "the rich" than any other group in society. "YouGov / Sunday Times Survey Results", *YouGov Plc.*, 9-10 April 2010 <www.yougov.co.uk>; "Brown Eton class comment spiteful, says Cameron", *BBC News*, 6 December 2009; "Tessa Jowell warns against election 'class war'", *BBC News*, 27 December 2009

10   Andrew Porter & Caroline Gammell, "Anthony Steen: 'voters are just jealous of my very, very large house' - MPs' expenses", *Daily Telegraph*, 22 May 2009

11   Ian Kirby & Alex Clarke, "WestMINTster: 19 of the 29 Shadow Cabinet members are MILLIONAIRES", *News of the World*, 29 July 2008; Gerri Peev, "Cameron forces his shadow cabinet to give up 'millionaires' row' jobs", *Scotsman*, 20 June 2009

12   Dylan Jones, *Cameron on Cameron: Conversations With Dylan Jones*, Fourth Estate, London, 2008, p. 35

13   To this Marxian account of class, one might add a refinement drawn from Ralf Dahrendorf. The 'right to manage' alludes to a power relationship in the workplace, in which an expanding layer of managers exercises authority on behalf of capital, and perhaps share in some of the surplus generated by it, without themselves owning any. This layer has been called the 'new middle class', in contrast to the 'old middle class' of professionals and sole traders. See Reese Vanneman & Lynn Weber Cannon, *The*

American Perception of Class, Temple University Press, Philadelphia, 1987; and Robert V Robinson & Jonathan Kelley, "Class as Conceived by Marx and Dahrendorf: Effects on Income Inequality and Politics in the United States and Great Britain", *American Sociological Review*, Vol. 44, No. 1, February 1979, pp. 38-58

14   Understanding class in this way helps to explain why Gordon Brown's attempted jibe at Cameron's Eton education was such a fumbled pass. Brown wished to invoke the "old boys' network" that he supposes rankles with the 'meritocratic' instincts of swing voters. But though Cameron is of the aristocratic caste, his success has been achieved in capitalist terms. His tuition was paid for by his father's success as precisely the sort of "wealth creator" that New Labour has celebrated since its inception, and still does. This is, after all, a party that is "intensely relaxed about people getting filthy rich" (dixit Peter Mandelson).

15   "Young pretender?", interview with Andrew Marr, *BBC Sunday AM*, 9 October 2005; Dylan Jones, *Cameron on Cameron: Conversations With Dylan Jones*, Fourth Estate, London, 2008, p. 34

16   Robert Booth, "Who is behind the Taxpayers' Alliance?", *The Guardian*, 9 October 2009

17   Steve Schifferes, "Flat tax inventor turned critic", *BBC News*, 10 October 2005

18   Tax Reform Commission, HM Treasury, 2006: <http://www.hm-treasury.gov.uk/d/foi_taxreformcom _06.pdf>; see also Allister Heath, *Flat Tax: Towards a British Model*, Stockholm Network, 2006, available online: <http://tpa.typepad.com/research/files/flattax.pdf>

19   Tax Reform Commission, HM Treasury, 2006: <http://www.hm-treasury.gov.uk/d/foi_taxreformcom_ 06.pdf>;

20   Jo Blanden & Stephen Machin, "Recent Changes in

Intergenerational Mobility in Britain", Sutton Trust, December 2007 <http://www2.lse.ac.uk/intranet/LSE Services/divisionsAndDepartments/ERD/pressAndInforma tionOffice/PDF/Recent%20Changes%20in%20Intergenerati onal%20Mobility%20in%20Britain.pdf>

21 Charlotte Denny, "Privately financed revolution", *The Guardian*, 3 October 2002; see Allyson Pollock, *NHS PLc: The Privatization of Our Healthcare*, Verso Books, London & New York, 2004; Allyson Pollock, 'The exorbitant cost of PFI is now being cruelly exposed', *The Guardian*, 26 January 2006

22 Andy McSmith, "Cameron: I'll give power to the petition", *The Independent*, 9 February 2010

Chapter One

23 See, for example, Stephen Cushion, "Protesting their Apathy? An Analysis of British Press Coverage of Young anti-Iraq War Protestors", *Journal of Youth Studies*, Vol. 10, No. 4, September 2007, pp. 419-437; also recall the "spurious cause" which Tony Blair said motivated anticapitalist protesters.

24 Ron Johnson & Charles Pattie, *Putting voters in their place: geography and elections in Great Britain*, Oxford University Press, 2006 , p. 246

25 Reeve Vannerman & Lynn Weber Cannon, *The American Perception of Class*, Temple University Press, 1987, pp. 164-166

26 Ron Johnson & Charles Pattie, *Putting voters in their place: geography and elections in Great Britain*, Oxford University Press, 2006, p. 7; Anthony F Heath, Roger M Jowell & John K Curtice, "Were Traditional Labour Voters Disillusioned with New Labour ?", *The Rise of New Labour*, 2001, pp. 147-56; Susan Watkins, "A Weightless Hegemony: New Labour's Role in the Neoliberal Economy", *New Left Review* 25, January/February 2004; Pippa Norris, "Apathetic Landslide:

The 2001 British General Election", *Parliamentary Affairs* 54, 2001, pp. 565-589

27 Stephen Driver & Luke Martell, *New Labour*, Polity Press, 2006, p. 21; Ron Johnson & Charles Pattie, *Putting voters in their place: geography and elections in Great Britain*, Oxford University Press, 2006, pp. 29-30. A caveat is in order here. Most pollsters use a definition of class that is predicated on lifestyle or status indicators, or they use the occupation-based categories from the National Readership Survey. These are at best proxies for class, and at times rather poor ones. First of all, NRS surveys tend to underestimate the number of poor, unemployed and benefit-dependent workers in society because they ask only about the chief income earner in each household. That may be appropriate where households had only one real bread-winner, but not when households depend on all adults being in employment. One such survey by Ipsos Mori estimated that 8% of the population aged 15+ belonged to social grade E – this includes all those on benefits, as well as casual and 'lowest grade' workers and state pensioners. 8% of people aged 15+ in the UK is approximately 4 million. But in the year the survey was conducted, there were over 5 million people on job-seekers and disability benefits alone. A further 1.3 million lived on the state pension, and 3.25 million worked in the most 'elementary' occupations. A total of 9 million people arguably belonged to category E, but less than half of them were detected. See 'Social Grade: A Classification Tool', Ipsos-Mori, July 2009: <http://www.ipsos-mori.com/DownloadPublication/ 1285_MediaCT_thoughtpiece_Social_Grade_July09_V3_W EB.pdf>. Secondly, their classifications are not connected to the distribution of power and wealth in society, which I have earlier insisted is essential to the proper definition of class. Thus, voters belonging to social grade C1 include a

high quotient of clerical workers and call centre employees who are thereby classified as belonging to the 'lower middle class', though they have little in common with the shopkeepers and cabbies, or self-employed plumbers, electricians and carpenters who are traditionally identified with the lower middle class. Nor do they have a share of power in the workplace, as members of the 'new middle class' such as junior managers and supervisors do.

28 Daron Acemoglu & James A Robinson, "Why Did the West Extend the Franchise? Democracy, Inequality and Growth in Historical Perspective", MIT Press, 1998, available online: <http://web.mit.edu/daron/www/qje_kuz6.pdf>; Their argument overlaps in important ways with that of Paul Foot, the campaigning journalist and socialist, whose posthumously published account of the struggle for the vote is the finest to date. See Paul Foot, *The Vote: How it was Won and How it was Undermined*, Penguin Viking, 2005

29 John Ramsden, Appetite *for Power: A History of the Conservative Party Since 1830*, HarperCollins, 1998, p. 93; Chris Williams, *A companion to nineteenth-century Britain*, Wiley-Blackwell, 2004, p. 170

30 John Ramsden, *Appetite for Power: A History of the Conservative Party Since 1830*, HarperCollins, 1998, p. 243

31 Paul Foot, *The Vote: How it was Won and How it was Undermined*, Penguin Viking, 2005, pp. 286-288

32 Paul Mason, *Live Working and Die Fighting: How the Working Class Went Global*, Vintage Books, London, 2008

33 See Ralph Miliband, *Capitalist Democracy in Britain*, Oxford Paperbacks, 1984; Ralph Miliband, *The State in Capitalist Society: The Analysis of the Western System of Power*, Open University, 1969; and for an overview of the Milibandian critique of parliamentary socialism and the Labour Party, see David Coates, ed., *Paving The Third Way: The Critique of Parliamentary Socialism*, Merlin Press, London, 2003

34 See *Paul Foot, The Vote: How It Was Won And How It Was Undermined,* Penguin Viking, 2005, pp. 306-310

35 See "NHS attack by MEP 'unpatriotic'", *BBC News*, 14 August 2009 <http://news.bbc.co.uk/1/hi/uk_politics/8200817.stm>

36 Brian Watkin, *Documents on health and social services, 1834 to the present day*, Methuen, 1975, pp. 93-96

37 Tony Cliff and Donny Gluckstein, *The Labour Party: A Marxist History*, Bookmarks, London, Chicago & Sydney, 1996, p. 253

38 See Larry Elliott and Dan Atkinson, *The Age of Insecurity*, Verso, London & New York, 1999

39 Gregory Elliott, *Labourism and the English Genius: The Strange Death of Labour England?*, Verso, London and New York, 1993, pp. 57-59

40 Alasdair Macintyre, "From MacDonald to Gaitskell", in Paul Blackledge and Neil Davidson, eds., *Alasdair Macintyre's Engagement With Marxism*, Haymarket Books, Chicago, 2005, pp. 110-111; Stuart Weir and David Beetham, *Political Power and Democratic Control in Britain*, Routledge, 1998, pp. 33-36

41 Ralph Miliband, *The State in Capitalist Society*, Quartet Books, 1969, p. 97; Gregory Elliott, *Labourism and the English Genius: The Strange Death of Labour England?*, Verso, London and New York, 1993, pp. 57-58

42 Gregory Elliott, *Labourism and the English Genius: The Strange Death of Labour England?*, Verso, London and New York, 1993, pp. 61-65

43 See David Coates, "The Failure of the Socialist Promise", in David Coates, ed., *Paving The Third Way: The Critique of Parliamentary Socialism*, Merlin Press, 2003, pp. 137-154

44 Anthony Seldon and Kevin Hickson, *New Labour, old Labour: the Wilson and Callaghan governments, 1974-79*, Routledge, 2004, pp. 207-208

45   See Andrew Gamble, "Neoliberalism", *Capital & Class* 75, 2001; and Andrew Glyn, *Capitalism Unleashed: Finance, Globalization and Welfare,* Oxford University Press, 2006

46   Hugh Parker Atkinson and Stuart Wilks-Heeg, *Local government from Thatcher to Blair: the politics of creative autonomy,* Wiley-Blackwell, 2000, pp. 57-59; James M Buchanan and Gordon Tullock, *The calculus of consent: logical foundations of constitutional democracy,* University of Michigan Press, 1962

47   See Wendy Brown's exceptional essay, "Neo-liberalism and the End of Liberal Democracy", *Theory and Event* 7:1, 2003; also, Wendy Brown, 'American Nightmare: Neoliberalism, Neoconservatism, and De-democratization', *Political Theory* 34, 2006

48   Andrew Gamble, "THE FREE ECONOMY AND THE STRONG STATE:THE RISE OF THE SOCIAL MARKET ECONOMY", *Socialist Register,* 1979

49   Ludwig von Mises, *Liberalism: The Classical Tradition,* Liberty Fund Inc, 2005, p. 30; See Perry Anderson, "The Intransigent Right" in *Spectrum: from right to left in the world of ideas,* Verso, 2005, pp. 13-15; Richard M Ebeling, "Globalisation and the International Market Place", in Peter J Boettke & Peter T Leeson, *The legacy of Ludwig Von Mises,* Edward Elgar Publishing Ltd, 2006

50   See Perry Anderson, "The Intransigent Right" in *Spectrum: from right to left in the world of ideas,* Verso, 2005, pp. 15-16; Renée Sallas, "Friedrich von Hayek, Leader and Master of Liberalism", *El Mercurio,* 12 April 1981. Transcript available at: <http://www.fahayek.org/index.php?option=com_cont ent&task=view&id=121>; On the influence of the Chicago Boys in Chile, see David Harvey, *Neoliberalism: A Short History,* Oxford University Press, 2005, pp. 7-9; Naomi Klein, *The Shock Doctrine: The Rise of Disaster Capitalism,* Metropolitan Books, New York, 2007, pp. 77-87; Greg

Grandin, 'The Road From Serfdom: Milton Friedman and the Economics of Empire', *Counterpunch*, 17 November 2006

51 John Saville, "AN OPEN CONSPIRACY: CONSERVATIVE POLITICS AND THE MINERS' STRIKE 1984-5", *Socialist Register*, 1985

52 Seumas Milne, *The Enemy Within: The Secret War Against the Miners*, Verso, London & New York, 2004

53 Tim Bale, *The Conservative Party: From Thatcher to Cameron*, Polity, 2010, p. 23

54 See, for example, Johann Hari, "The forces blocking British democracy", *The Independent*, 23 April 2010

55 Perry Anderson, *The New Old World*, Verso, London & New York, 2009, pp. 156-157 & 169-170

56 David Coates, *Prolonged Labour: The Slow Birth of Labour Britain*, Palgrave Macmillan, 2005, p. 8; Maurice Mullard, *The Politics of Public Expenditure*, Routledge, 1993, p. 222; Harry Wallop, "Individual share ownership falls to all-time low", *Daily Telegraph*, 27 January 2010; Paul Wilenius, "Enemies within: Thatcher and the unions", *BBC News*, 5 March 2004

57 Luc Boltanski and Eve Chiapello, *The New Spirit of Capitalism*, Verso, London & New York, 2007. I am grateful to Jeremy Gilbert for discussing this subject with me. His argument regarding the 'new spirit' of capitalism can be found in "After '68: Narratives of the New Capitalism", *New Formations*, 2008

58 Anthony Heath, Roger Jowell and John Curtice, "UNDER-STANDING ELECTORAL CHANGE IN BRITAIN", *Parliamentary Affairs*, Oxford University Press, 1986; Eric Hobsbawm, *Politics for a Rational Left*, Verso, London & New York, 1989, p. 164

59 Perry Anderson, *Spectrum: from right to left in the world of ideas*, Verso, London & New York, 2005, p. 289; Eric

Hobsbawm, *Politics for a Rational Left*, Verso, London & New York, 1989, pp. 63-99

60   Tony Cliff and Donny Gluckstein, *The Labour Party: a Marxist history*, Bookmarks, London, Chicago & Sydney, 1996, pp. 345-355

61   Anthony Heath, Roger Jowell and John Curtice, "UNDER-STANDING ELECTORAL CHANGE IN BRITAIN", *Parliamentary Affairs*, Oxford University Press, 1986

62   Again, see Wendy Brown, "Neo-liberalism and the End of Liberal Democracy", *Theory and Event* 7:1, 2003

Chapter Two

63   Gordon Brown, "We can break the glass ceiling", *The Guardian*, 15 January 2010

64   Harold James Perkin, *The Third Revolution: professional elites in the modern world*, Routledge, 1996, pp. 77-78

65   See especially Paine's extemporisation on the principle of heredity in the pamphlet, Common Sense. Thomas Paine, *Rights of Man, Common Sense, and Other Political Writings*, Penguin, 1995, pp. 15-18

66   Quoted in Stephen J MacNamee & Robert K Miller Jr., *The Meritocracy Myth*, Rowman & Littlefied, 2004, p. 7

67   For a discussion of conservative attempts to galvanise the desire for distinction into support for hierarchy, including slavery, see Corey Robin, 'Out of Place', *The Nation*, 4 June 2008

68   James Kirkup, "David Cameron pledges 'brazen elitism' in teaching", *Daily Telegraph*, 18 January 2010; Richard Preston, "As Carol Vorderman knows, there's no shame in taking a Thora", *Daily Telegraph*, 19 January 2010

69   For their part, Wilkinson and Pickett were less than joyous to find their work being cited by Cameron, pointing out that Thatcher had laid the basis for the 'broken society' that Cameron bewailed. Richard Wilkinson and Kate Pickett, "A

broken society, yes. But broken by Thatcher", *The Guardian*, 29 January 2010

70 Andrew Sparrow, "Parental 'warmth' more important than wealth, says David Cameron", *The Guardian*, 11 January 2010. Cameron misrepresented the research upon which he had based his claims. See Polly Toynbee, "Little by little, the blue seeps through Cameron's silky skin", *The Guardian*, 11 January 2010; on the Tories' tax proposed tax changes, see Nigel Morris, "Tories announce £150 tax break for four million married couples", *The Independent*, 10 April 2010

71 See Val Gillies, "Raising the 'Meritocracy: Parenting and the Individualization of Social Class", *Sociology*, Vol. 39, No. 5, 2005

72 See Frank O'Gorman, *Edmund Burke: his political philosophy*, Routledge, , pp. 45-47 & 120-122

73 See Joseph Romance & Neal Riemer, *Democracy and Excellence: concord or conflict?*, Greenwood Publishing, 2005

74 Friedrich Nietzsche, *Thus Spake Zarathustra*, The Echo Library, 2009, p. 21; Friedrich Nietzsche, *Beyond Good and Evil*, Cambridge University Press, 2002, p. 151. It is not difficult to imagine Nietzsche's scorn, either, for the managerial mediocrity that generally passes for 'excellence' in this era.

75 Friedrich Hayek, *The Road to Serfdom*, Routledge, 2001, p 169; Friedrich Hayek, *The Constitution of Liberty*, University of Chicago, 1960, pp. 128-130

76 Ayn Rand, *The Fountainhead*, Abe Books, 1993, pp. 635 & 639

77 I am grateful to Corey Robin for this argument.

78 See Ted Honderich's discussion of this argument in *Conservatism: Burke, Nozick, Bush, Blair?*, Pluto Press, London, Ann Arbor, 2005, pp. 45-50

79 Quoted by Ted Honderich, *Conservatism: Burke, Nozick,*

Bush, Blair?, Pluto Press, London, Ann Arbor, 2005, p. 9

80 Karl Mannheim, "The Democratization of Culture", in Kurt H Wolff, ed., *From Karl Mannheim*, Transaction Books, 1993, p. 480

81 Michael Young, *The Rise of the Meritocracy*, Transaction Books, 2004

82 Alan O Ebenstein, *Friedrich Hayek: A Biography*, University of Chicago Press, 2003, pp. 291-292

83 Friedrich Hayek, *The Constitution of Liberty*, University of Chicago, 1960, pp. 88-89; The insistence that talent is undeserved is where John Rawls' theory of justice scandalises right-wing liberals such as Nozick. See Alex Callinicos, *Equality*, Polity, 2000, pp. 46-48

84 Margaret Thatcher, Speech to the Institute of Socio-Economic Studies ("Let Our Children Grow Tall"), New York, 15 September 1975, reproduced at: <http://www.margaretthatcher.org/speeches/displaydocument.asp?docid=102769>

85 Margaret Thatcher, House of Commons speech, Her Majesty's Government Opposition Motion (motion of no confidence), 23 March 1977: <http://www.margaretthatcher.org/speeches/displaydocument.asp?docid=103344>

86 Margaret Thatcher, "Interview for The Sun", 28 February 1983: <http://www.margaretthatcher.org/speeches/displaydocument.asp?docid=105089>

87 Rebecca Surender and Jane Lewis, *Welfare state change: towards a Third Way?*, Oxford University Press, 2004, pp. 35-36; Larry Elliott and Dan Atkinson, *The Age of Insecurity*, Verso, London & New York, 1999, pp. 232-233

88 Quoted, Claire Charlot, Monica Charlot, Bernard d' Hellencourt, *New Britain: key documents*, Ophrys, 2002, pp. 47-48

89 Mary Riddell, "Statisticians tell us that we're all middle class now - but that doesn't stop poorer people dying

younger", *New Statesman*, 4 December 1998. According to the 2007 British Social Attitudes Survey, 57% of people identified as working class in 2005, only a slight fall on 1983, when 61% self-identified as working class, and the change was attributed largely to the absence in 2005 of prominent class-based social conflicts. Neither Thatcher nor Blair had been able to persuade people that they were part of a protean and dynamic new middle class. Curiously, the fact that a majority as working class, and a minority as middle class, has been taken as proof of the assertion that we're all middle class now. See Judith Woods, "We're all middle class now, darling", *Daily Telegraph*, 22 January 2010

90 Andrew Grice, "We are wealth creators now, says Labour", *The Independent*, 2 February 1999

91 Greg Philo & David Miller, *Market Killing: What the Free Market does and what social scientists can do about it*, Pearson Books, 2000, pp. 18-19

92 Alex Callinicos, *Against the Third Way*, Polity Press, 2001, pp. 62-67

93 Stephen Aldridge, "Social Mobility: A Discussion Paper", Performance and Innovation Unit, HM Government, April 2001: <http://www.cabinetoffice.gov.uk/media/cabinet office/strategy/assets/socialmobility.pdf>; Alex Callinicos, "Meritocracy: Unequal Opportunities", Socialist Review, June 2001

94 Michael Young, "Down with meritocracy", *The Guardian*, 29 June 2001

95 "A Bit Rich: Calculating the real value to society of different professions", *New Economics Foundation*, December 2009: <http://www.neweconomics.org/sites/neweconomics.org/fi les/A_Bit_Rich.pdf>

96 Mike Brewer, Alastair Muriel, David Phillips & Luke Sibieta, "Poverty and Income Inequality in the UK: 2009", Institute for Fiscal Studies, May 2009 <http://www.ifs.org

.uk/comms/c109.pdf>; Philip Inman, "Labour's tax and benefits strategy has closed the income gap, thinktank says", *The Guardian*, 25 March 2010

97 Alex Callinicos, *Against the Third Way*, Polity Press, 2001, pp. 48-51; Andrew Glyn, *Capitalism Unleashed*, Oxford University Press, 2006, pp. 7 & 116-117 & 190-191; David Hencke, "PM facing battle with unions over EU treaty", *The Guardian*, 23 August 2007; Blair quoted in John Hendy, "A crime in the world's eyes", *New Statesman*, 13 September 2004

98 John Plender, "Love affair with the rich is well and truly dead", *Financial Times*, 24 March 2010

99 Andrew Lloyd Webber, "The last thing this country needs is a pirate raid on the wealth creators who still dare navigate our stormy waters (...And don't lynch me as a rich b*****d flying a kite for his own cause - I really fear an exodus of talent)", *Daily Mail*, 27 April 2009

100 Richard Woods, 'The Sunday Times Rich List 2010: fortunes of super-rich soar by a third', *The Sunday Times*, 25 April 2010

101 Jack Grimston, "Ex-minister wants young jobless starved into work", *Sunday Times*, 25 April 2010

Chapter Three

102 Dylan Jones, *Cameron on Cameron: Conversations with Dylan Jones*, Fourth Estate, London, 2008, p. 107

103 Ted Honderich, *Conservatism: Burke, Nozick, Bush, Blair?*, Pluto Press, London, Ann Arbor, 2005, pp. 7-8

104 C Wright Mills, "The Conservative Mood", *Dissent*, Winter 1954; Karl Mannheim, "Conservative Thought", in Kurt H Wolff, ed., *From Karl Mannheim*, Transaction Books, 1993, pp. 270-281

105 Corey Robin, "Conservatives", unpublished essay; see also Corey Robin, "Out of Place", *The Nation*, 4 June 2008. I am

grateful to Corey for discussing his ideas with me.

106 Dan Hind, *The Threat to Reason*, Verso, London & New York, 2007

107 Perry Anderson, *The Origins of Postmodernity*, Verso, London & New York, 1998, p. 66

108 Anthony Giddens, *Beyond Left and Right: The future of radical politics*, Stanford University Press, 1994

109 See Alex Callinicos on Fukuyama as an exponent of *kulturkritik*, and on his left-wing sympathisers. *Theories and Narratives*, Polity Press, 1995, pp. 15-43

110 Anthony Seldon, *Blair*, The Free Press, 2005, pp. 119-137

111 See Frances Stonor Saunders, *Who Paid the Piper?: CIA and the Cultural Cold War*, Granta Books, 1999; and Hugh Wilford, *The CIA, the British left, and the Cold War: calling the tune?*, Frank Cass Publishers, 2003; Robin Ramsay, *The Rise of New Labour*, Pocket Essentials, 2002; Andy Beckett, "Friends in high places", *The Guardian*, 6 November 2004; Anthony Seldon, *Blair*, The Free Press, 2005, pp. 119-137

112 For a discussion of the social interests and blocs involved in the 1984 Democratic campaign, see Manning Marable, "Race and Realignment in American Politics", in Manning Marable, *Beyond Black and White: Transforming African-American Politics*, Verso, London & New York, 1996, pp. 26-33

113 See Christopher Hitchens, *No One Left To Lie To: The Values of the Worst Family*, Verso, London & New York, pp. 59-65; Bill Clinton, "How We Ended Welfare, Together", *New York Times*, 22 August 2006

114 Theda Skocpol, "Democrats at the Cross Roads", *Mother Jones*, February 1997, pp. 54-59

115 Quoted in Alex Callinicos, *Against the Third Way*, Polity, 2001, pp. 23-24

116 Stephen Driver, "'Fixing Our Broken Society': David Cameron's Post-Thatcherite Social policy'" , in Simon Lee

and Matt Beech, eds., *The Conservatives Under David Cameron: Built to Last?*, Palgrave Macmillan, 2009, p. 83

117 "Tony Blair's speech in full", *BBC News*, 28 September 1999; Tony Blair, quoted in Anthony Giddens, *The Third Way*, Polity Press, 2000, p. 1

118 John Maynard Keynes, *The General Theory of Employment, Interest and Money*, Atlantic Publishing, 2006, p. 351

119 See Chris Harman, "Globalisation: A Critique of a New Orthodoxy", *International Socialism* 73, 1996

120 Tony Blair, "Doctrine of the International Community", Chicago, 24 April 1999: <http://webarchive.nation-alarchives.gov.uk/+/http://www.number10.gov.uk/Page1297>

121 See Richard Seymour, *The Liberal Defence of Murder*, Verso, London & New York, 2008

122 Quoted in Tom Bentley, "Can the Centre Hold? British Politics After Tony Blair", *British Politics*, Vol. 2, 2007

123 David Coates, *Prolonged Labour: The Slow Birth of New Labour Britain*, Palgrave Macmillan, 2005, pp. 116-117

124 For a comparison of the 2010 manifesto with its predecessors, see Nigel Morris, "Tory manifesto: The case for the big society", *The Independent*, 14 April 2010; on the Tories wafer-thin critique of New Labour's handling of the civil service, see Francis Maude, "Labour has tainted the civil service", *The Guardian*, 8 February 2010

125 Phillip Blond, "Rise of the red Tories", *Prospect*, 28 February 2009

126 Nathan Coombs, "The Political Theology of Red Toryism", PSA Annual Conference, Edinburgh, 2010

127 Phillip Blond and Adrian Pabst, "The roots of Islamic terrorism", *New York Times*, 28 July 2005; Philip Blond and Adrian Pabst, "Integrating Islam into the West", *New York Times*, 4 November 2008

128 Jonathan Raban, "Cameron's Crank", *London Review of*

Books, Vol. 32, No. 8, 22 April 2010

129 Nathan Coombs, "The Political Theology of Red Toryism", PSA Annual Conference, Edinburgh, 2010; I am grateful to Corey Robin for discussing these ideas with me.

130 Mark Evans, "Cameron's Competition State", in Simon Lee and Matt Beech, eds., *The Conservatives Under David Cameron: Built to Last?*, Palgrave Macmillan, 2009

131 See David Judge, "Whatever Happened to Parliamentary Democracy in the United Kingdom?", *Parliamentary Affairs*, Vol. 57, No. 3, 2004

132 Klaus Dodds and Stuart Elden, "Thinking Ahead: David Cameron, the Henry Jackson Society and British Neo-conservatism", *British Journal of Politics and International Relations*, Vol. 10, 2008

133 Victoria Honeyman, "David Cameron and Foreign and International Policy", in Simon Lee and Matt Beech, eds., *The Conservatives Under David Cameron: Built to Last?*, Palgrave Macmillan, 2009, pp. 173-176

134 Michael Gove, "I can't fight my feelings any more: I love Tony", *The Times*, 25 February 2003

135 On Bogdanor, see Frances Elliott and James Hanning, *Cameron: The Rise of the New Conservative*, Fourth Estate, 2007, p. 67

136 Klaus Dodds and Stuart Elden, "Thinking Ahead: David Cameron, the Henry Jackson Society and British Neo-conservatism", *British Journal of Politics and International Relations*, Vol. 10, 2008; Anita Singh, "Tony Blair: Iraq War was right even if there were no WMDs", *Daily Telegraph*, 12 December 2009

137 Frances Elliott and James Hanning, *Cameron: The Rise of the New Conservative*, Fourth Estate, 2007, pp. 208-211; David Cameron, 'Time to be counted', *The Guardian*, 17 March 2003

Conclusion

138 David Harvey, *A Brief History of Neoliberalism*, Oxford University Press, 2005, pp. 31-36

139 Andrew Denham & Keiron O'Hara, "Cameron's 'Mandate': Democracy, Legitimacy and Conservative Leadership", *Parliamentary Affairs*, 2007

140 Larry Elliott, "Mervyn King warned that election victor will be out of power for a generation, claims economist", *The Guardian*, 29 April 2010; John Lanchester, "The Great British Economy Disaster", *London Review of Books*, Vol. 3, No. 5, 11 March 2010

141 Larry Elliott, "A few strikes don't make a spring of discontent", *The Guardian*, 29 March 2010; Ruth Sunderland, "Invasion of the booty snatchers: how greed is spreading out from the City", *The Observer*, 18 October 2010; Ruth Sunderland, "Unemployment across UK is back to 1999 levels", *The Observer*, 18 April 2010; "Labour Market Statistics", *Human Resources Management Guide*, 17 March 2010; Andrew Porter, "Labour warns that unemployment will rise this year", *Daily Telegraph*, 1 February 2010; Richard Woods, "The Sunday Times Rich List 2010: fortunes of super-rich soar by a third", *Sunday Times*, 25 April 2010

142 "Osborne launches white paper on financial regulation", *Conservatives.com*, 20 July 2009

143 On Britain's vulnerability to speculative attack, see Larry Elliott, "The UK isn't so different from Greece: a financial crisis could happen here too", *The Guardian*, 19 April 2010; On the possibility of default, see investment analyst Marc Faber, "US, Europe Will All Default On Their Debt: Marc Faber", *CNBC*, 10 February 2010; Larry Rohter, "Chile's Candidates Agree to Agree on Pension Woes", *New York Times*, 10 January 2006; Robin Blackburn, "A GLOBAL PENSION PLAN", *New Left Review* 47, September-October

2007; Larry Rohter, "Chile's Retirees Find Shortfall in Private Plan", *New York Times*, 27 January 2005; Robin Blackburn, *Age shock: how finance is failing us*, Verso, London & New York, 2007, p. 99

144 Melanie Lansbury, "UK manufacturing employment since Beveridge: the chemical and motor vehicle industries", National Institute of Economic and Social Research, August 1995 ; "Manufacturing Statistics 2009", Institute for Manufacturing, September 2009 <http://www.ifm.eng.cam.ac.uk/cig/09stats/workforce.html>; David Coates, *Prolonged Labour: The Slow Birth of New Labour Britain*, Palgrave Macmillan, 2005, pp 8-11 & 17-18

Contemporary culture has eliminated both the concept of the public and the figure of the intellectual. Former public spaces – both physical and cultural – are now either derelict or colonized by advertising. A cretinous anti-intellectualism presides, cheerled by expensively educated hacks in the pay of multinational corporations who reassure their bored readers that there is no need to rouse themselves from their interpassive stupor. The informal censorship internalized and propagated by the cultural workers of late capitalism generates a banal conformity that the propaganda chiefs of Stalinism could only ever have dreamt of imposing. Zer0 Books knows that another kind of discourse – intellectual without being academic, popular without being populist – is not only possible: it is already flourishing, in the regions beyond the striplit malls of so-called mass media and the neurotically bureaucratic halls of the academy. Zer0 is committed to the idea of publishing as a making public of the intellectual. It is convinced that in the unthinking, blandly consensual culture in which we live, critical and engaged theoretical reflection is more important than ever before.